Makarand Arvind Paithankar

Human Resource in Government

Policies and Practices in India

ISBN-13: 978- 1534998391

ISBN-10: 153499839X

Made by: CreateSpace
        4900 LaCross Road
        North Charleston, SC 29406
        USA

First print July 2016

CONTENTS

Preface

For me it is deeply satisfying experience to present this work. The most significant asset to an organization is its people. This book is intended for those who have general interest in the working of human element in organization and especially in government domain. This book attempts to satisfy the needs of scholars and also the students pursuing public administration, government and policy studies. The book is comprehensive yet concise picture of a very vital subject of study.

This book is planned in fifteen parts covering important aspects of human resource in government like classification, recruitment, training, promotion, retirement-benefits, and also the issues like discipline, neutrality, anonymity, generalists and specialists. The book also discuss in detail bureaucracy, civil service in India and employee-employer mechanism.

I am indebted to large numbers of scholars and authors upon whose writings I have largely drawn. To those who took the trouble to read the manuscript and offer comments I am grateful. I would like to thank my Management where I work; and to colleagues and friends, discussions with whom have always enriched my points of view. Thanks to CreateSpace for taking up this work.

Finally I thank my wife Smita and son Raghav for their continued support.

INTRODUCTION

The Personnel is sovereign. If men and women are competent enough, they can give life even to inexact, confused, and rough-hewn demarcations. Personnel is the sovereign factor in public administration Will and mind are first; they engender policy; and mechanism is subsidiary to function[1]

The study of human resource in government is variously known as personnel administration, personnel management, and human resource management. In public administration literature it is used interchangeably and many times synonymously. Tead Ordway and Henry C. Metcalf used it in 1920, they wrote, "Personnel administration" is used...synonymously with "employment administration," "personnel management," "administration of human relations," and "administration of industrial relations." And we shall, in referring to the staff department which performs this function, use all of these names interchangeably. In referring to the administrative divisions of this department which undertake specific work such as employment, training, research, service, etc., we shall speak of them as "divisions," "bureaus" or "sections." If we have occasion to use the term "employment manager," it will be to designate the head of the employment division; similarly the term "service" or "welfare manager"

1

will mean the head of the service division. Personnel administration is the direction and coordination of the human relations of any organization with a view to getting the maximum necessary production with a minimum of effort and friction, and with proper regard for the genuine well-being of the workers.[2]

By the 19th century the civil service commission in 1855 on the background of the Northcote-Trevelyan Report of 1854 established civil services in Britain and the Pendleton Act of 1883 did it in the US. After that world witnessed the gradual emergence of the civil services, the personnel profession began to take on different functions in the classification, recruitment and promotion of public employees.

Before the nineteenth century most civil servants were chosen upon what have been called, not always appropriately, political grounds. That is, most public appointments were made on the basis of partisanship, influence, wealth, family, personal loyalty, blackmail, or charity, rather than intelligence or competence to do their work[3]

In the literature of public administration this view of human resource management is succinctly put forth by Frederick Mosher in his synthesis of Brownlow committee report of 1937. It highlights the rule and procedural orientation of personnel administration, neglecting efficient and effective functioning of the public administration. He writes, "Personnel administration lies at the very core of administrative management. Its thrust should be positive and substantive, not negative and protective, not specialized and procedural as had been the emphasis of the predecessor civil service movements...It should operate primarily as a service to managers up and down the line, not as a watchdog and controller over management... Personnel operations...should be decentralized and delegated to bring them into more immediate relationship with the middle and lower managers whom they serve."[4]

The administration of traditional merit systems is the central idea of public personnel's main function with time this idea has been substituted by 'all inclusive' human resource management view. The National Academy of Public Administration makes note of the changing public sector environment, first, the nature of work and the workplace are dramatically changing due to technological advances, the ability to develop and access vast amounts of data, and the need to communicate more rapidly and on more levels than ever before. Second, expectations of the workforce reflect differences in generational attitudes toward work and careers, adding another dimension to the challenge of managing a diverse workforce. Third, the shape of the workforce is changing, emphasizing a more blended workforce of permanent civil servants, temporary and intermittent employees, and contractors using a continuous process of public/private competition.[5]

There are many authors particularly those who come from organization and management studies have brought out the development of the study of human resource in various stages, beginning from 1900. The stages that swayed the study and practice of the human element are

1900- Welfare stage: Period of industrialization, scientific development, and World War I created demand for production that necessitated welfare measures to be made available for employees.

1920-30- Personnel administration: Pressures to increase productivity, proliferation of organizations made it imperative to have recruitment, promotion that facilitated transition of welfare officer to personnel administrator.

1940-60- Personnel management: Context of great depression, period of world war II, new work demands, supervision, labour issues, all these challenged efficiency. Human relations school, behaviouralism had its influence. Centre of focus moved from individual to group, manpower planning, organization development, organization effectiveness, training, industrial relations evolved, customer care technological changes resulted into personnel management.

1970-90- Human resource management: Organizational excellence, macro approach quality, commitment, culture, change, proactive role became central theme for human resource management.

2000- Strategic human resource management: focus on employee management techniques that are directed towards gaining competitive advantage as a organizational strategy, systems that take care of individual employee and teams as vital assets, strategic approach and management practice for sustainable achievement of an organizational mission, goals, and objectives.

Still the definition of terms such as 'personnel management' and 'human resource management' is an area of confusion and irritation. I have used the phrase 'human resource' as a generic term that covers 'personnel administration/management' and 'human resource management.' However the differences and similarities presented by the scholars on the subject are presented here.

Similarities[6]

- Integration of policies with organisational goals
- Line management involvement in employee management
- Employee motivation and commitment
- Adding value

Differences[7]

Item	Personnel management	Human resource management
Goals and values	Incremental interventions in attracting retaining motivating workers	Strategic focus. competitiveness, profitability, survival, competitive advantage and workforce flexibility
Professionalism	Personnel managers are accountable for employees' matters (for which they are trained)	Line managers are accountable for their staff (they are multi-skilled)
Relations	Limited trust, conflict and differentiation, control oriented	Harmony, mutuality of interests, active employee involvement
Employee management	Narrow in focus, individualized	Broad and team focused
Information and communication	Control information and communication, bureaucratic, secretive	Transparency, objectivity, honesty, trust and commitment

The concept of government has metamorphosed and so with it our idea about civil service. In the new 'Governance' paradigm with its multifarious networking of public institutions, agencies, non government organizations, private sector engagement, civil service is one. This trends and transformations must be addressed in the study that involves 'Human' the vital resource of public organization. The concept of human resource management and the policies and practices of the government are alike in all but unimportant respects; it is substantially different in context, purpose and core values. The globalization has given momentum to more dynamic conceptualizations in public administration; the public – private divide is getting exceedingly blurred but one must keep in mind that the inherent *'loci'* of 'public agencies' is political in nature and hence it cannot be 'generic human resource management'. It is overall a study of policy and practice of human element in government domain.

POSITION CLASSIFICATION

Meaning

Modern Position classification, based on duties analysis, refers to the organizing of positions into groups or classes on the basis of their duties and qualification requirement.[8] Position classification is one of the most far reaching steps taken in public personnel field since the establishment of the civil service laws.[9] Position classification is a system of standardization and classification of government jobs to be integrated into an hierarchy. The Position classification movement in public sphere runs parallel with the job evaluation movement in the private business, 'the job is the thing' remains the main focus of both the movements. In position classification the actual position title corresponds to the duties one performs which not only clear confusion regarding position titles and fiscal control but is vital for personnel functions like recruitment, promotion, transfer, training, etc. Position classification laid the foundation for equitable treatment for public employees by the accurate definition, orderly arrangement, and fair evaluation of positions in the public service.[10] The subject of position classification is 'work performance', the process is 'work evaluation' and output of this arrangement of units of work into classes.

Classification Systems

Civil services are structured on two systems i.e. position classification and rank classification, there features are as under

Position classification	Rank classification
Organized around 'post' or position	Organized around member of 'service'
Hampers mobility as transfers are difficult	Intra-departmental transfers easy
Ideal for 'specialist' civil service	Ideal for 'generalist' civil service
Impersonal and objective in nature	Individual centric nature
Prevails in US, Canada, UN	It exists in England, India, Western Europe

Development of the Concept

Position classification evolved rapidly in US than elsewhere in the word. The reasons for its development are summarized as under

- The merit system required determination of job requirement and its classification
- The principle of 'equal pay for equal work' required jobs to be differentiated on the basis of requirements and specifications.

- The need for efficiency in the government required rationalization of job structure that is only possible through a systematic classification of job.

Advantages of Position Classification- The basic principles and uses of position classification are very well summarized by O. Glenn Stahl are[11]

1] Facilitating other personnel objectives

a. It provides a rational criterion for control of pay levels by making it possible to equate whole classes of positions with common salary ranges.

b. It reduces a variety of occupations and positions to manageable proportions so that recruitment, qualification requirements, examination, and selections can be made for whole classes of positions at a time.

c. It defines in objective terms the content of jobs (or what is expected) against which the performance of incumbents (how well it is done) can be measured.

d. It furnishes job information upon which the content of orientation and other in-service training can be based.

e. Although it does not for itself guarantee a good promotion and placement policy, it supplies a systematic picture of opportunities and position relationships, which is essential to an orderly promotion and placement procedure.

f. It provides a foundation for common understanding between supervisor and employee as to the job and pay, which facilitates employee management relation.

2] General aids to an organization

a. By use of standard class titles it establishes uniform job terminology.

b. It clarifies, by requiring definition and description of duties, the placing of responsibility in each position.

c. It provides an orderly basis for translating needs for positions into fiscal terms, thus facilitating budgetary procedures.

d. It provides information on job content that aids in the analysis of organizational problems and of procedures by bringing out points of duplication, inconsistency, and the like in the work process.

3] Particular value in Public service.

a. It assures the citizens and tax player that there is some logical relation between expenditures for personal services and the services rendered

b. It offers as good a protection as has been found against political or personal preferment in determination of public salaries.

The above mentioned two points assumes that the pay plan is determined by the system of position classification

Steps in Classification Plan

The characteristics of a classification plan includes[12]

1) Job description and analysis - analyzing and recording the duties and other distinctive characteristic of the position to be classified

2) Arranging positions into classes - Grouping the positions into classes upon the bases of their similarities.

3) Preparation of class standards - writing such standards or specifications for each class of positions as will indicate its character, define its boundaries, and serve as guide in allocating individual positions to the class and in recruitment and examinations.

4) Installation of the classification plan - It is of installation and administration by adoption of the plan; determination of agency to administer the plan; promulgation of the class standards; initial allocation of position to classes; adoption of formal rules for the administration of the classification; and provision for and hearing of appeals on allocations.

Essentials of Classification System

Fred Talford in his paper, the classification and salary standardization movement in the public service,[13] has enumerated the requirements for classification systems they are

- Collection of detailed facts with regard to the duties attached to each individual position with regard to its place

12

in the origination unit in which is occurs and with regard to functions organization and administrative procedure of organization unit.

- On the basis of this information a grouping of individual positions into classes.
- A written definition or description for each class of positions settings forth definitely the duties attached to the positions to be included in class.
- A written statement of minimum qualification which an individual must possess in order to perform duties of the position successfully.
- A title for each class of positions suggestive as far as possible of the duties attached to the positions in the organization unit in which is occur.
- On the basis of class definitions and defiance knowledge of the duties the allocation to the proper class of every position classified.
- The lines of promotion.
- The compensation schedules for each class giving maximum minimum and intermediate rates to be paid to the employees.
- To make the whole plan easily comprehensive a grouping of classes into broad occupational groups called services. Subdivided into grades according to the degree of

responsibility and therefore according to the level of compensation.

RECRUITMENT

Meaning

Recruitment is securing right people for right jobs and it may take the form of advertising for large groups of employees or tracking out a highly skilled individual for special work.[14] Recruitment is that process through which suitable candidates are induced to compete for appointments to the public service.[15] Recruitment is to attract the suitable proper candidate for the post to be filled up. Recruitment is vital process not only for the human management in the government but also for the entire administrative system. The quality of the public service and the caliber of its officers are determined by the recruitment. Recruitment is the gateway for aspirants of the civil services. The quality and soundness of governance in society depends on the principle of recruitment. No element of the personnel administration is as important as recruitment, as it is not repeated in the career span of an individual whereas the other elements like training, promotion, transfer are recurring in nature. As Stahl has rightly noted that the recruitment is the corner stone of the whole public personnel structure.

It was in ancient China that the recruitment system based on merit was introduced before Christ era in 2nd Century, but its modern form could be traced to Prussia. In India British introduced the merit system of recruitment in 1854 and one year later in 1855 it was introduced in Britain. In US with the assassination of President James Garfield in 1881 by Charles Guiteau a disappointed civil service aspirant resulted in introduction of merit system in place of spoils system with the enactment of Pendleton Civil Service Reform Act 1883.

Principles of Recruitment

1) Positive policy approach for recruitment.

2) Recruitment should draw most competent and best of the qualified persons.

3) Recruitment should provide maximum opportunity for the eligible to compete

4) Recruitment should be fair and non partisan.

5) Recruitment should be based on proper combinations of methods and techniques.

6) Recruitment should be dynamic and adaptable to changes of technology and modern times.

7) Recruitment should ensure right person for right job.

Forms of Recruitment

The recruitment system of any country is a thoughtful combination of the forms of recruitment. No system of recruitment subscribe to only one form. The forms of recruitment are discussed as under

Cadet System- This form of recruitment is generally followed in military. In this recruitment is made at the young age of 16-20 and the cadets are inculcated with the organization values. The 'catch them young' system help mould the cadets. The East India College, known popularly as the Haileybury College established in 1806 and closed for good in 1858 because of the introduction of merit, used to train officers of East India Company then known as 'Writers' in the same fashion. This form was also practiced by the Prussian government during the imperial era and by the erstwhile Soviet Union.

General Mental Culture - The form of recruitment first evolved in India during the British rule. The youths between the age group of 21-24 year are recruited on the basis of their broad cerebral accomplishments and mature mind and further they are given a continuous career of 30-35yrs. During this career span they draw long salary scales and get many promotions. In Indian variant of this form general educational background (any faculty) is considered while in Europe this form necessitates to have a degree in law.

Qualified and Skilled Matures- This form of recruitment is based on the position classification organized around post or positions available. Job specification and qualification criteria's are made explicit. Mature people between the age group of 18-45 year with special qualification and skills are recruited where usually long careers are not indicated. It is followed in US and Canada

Lateral Entry- Lateral entry is the form of recruitment normally considered for higher level positions. It is instilling talent from outside the civil service but with similar experiences or expertise in the relevant areas of the civil service. Lateral entry often takes place to recruit someone above the entry level because of the work experience of the person. The advantage of getting rightly qualified, senior and experienced persons in system is achieved by recruiting certain percentage of outsiders in senior positions.

Process of Recruitment

- Requisition for the demand for the jobs/posts
- Formulation of recruitment policy that includes eligibility conditions, qualifications, etc.
- Designing the application forms.
- Advertisement for the posts or examinations.
- Scrutiny of Applications.
- Conduct of exams, interviews, tests, etc.
- Evaluation process and results.
- Selection.
- Appointment by executive authority.
- Placement.

Location of Recruiting Authority

In democratic countries to ensure free and fair conduct of recruitment process largely depends on the recruiting authority. In most of the countries the authority for recruitment is vested in either semi independent or quasi judicial authorities or constitutional authorities. In USA it is the United States Merit Systems Protection Board, in UK it is Civil Service Commission, in India it is Public Service Commission.

Methods of Recruitment

The methods of recruitment followed in different countries in the world could be summarized as

- Direct recruitment and Indirect recruitment
- Positive and Negative Recruitment
- Mass Recruitment and Individual Recruitment.

Direct and Indirect Recruitment- The available positions in the government are filled by the most suitable of the available eligible candidates in open market then it is called as direct recruitment. This system gives maximum opportunity to all the eligible individuals and is in consonance with the democratic ethos. The best of the people are selected as the process is based on wide open competition. Direct recruitment brings in new ideas that reflect in the milieu of the services. Direct recruits are more adaptable to changes. It is hard work that is endured even in the civil service. The direct recruitment is not

19

flawless it has its disadvantages like lack of experience to hold responsible positions; training is imperative for direct recruits; hampers promotional prospects of in-service employees adversely affecting their efficiency and effectiveness; experience and hard is compromised.

The available positions in the government are filled by the most suitable of the available eligible candidates already in the service of the government then it is called as indirect recruitment. In other words promotion is indirect recruitment. Experienced individuals discharge duties confidently and responsibly. Long term training is not vital for individuals recruited by this method. Career progression and advancement creates the positive spell on the overall psyche of the employees. Hard work, loyalty and experience when rewarded results in increase in performance. Indirect recruitment reduces the burden of recruiting agency and it is also cost effective. Most of the employees will work hard for the better prospects it will make civil service an attractive career option. Career service without promotion cannot exist. The disadvantages are it gives opportunity to limited individuals; few available alternatives for the post; new blood are deprived of chance to enter the services' results in complacency and conservatism; reduces dynamism; makes civil service outdated; employee becomes opportunity mongers.

The best method of recruitment is the judicious mix of both the direct and indirect recruitment. Entry level positions are normally filled by direct method of recruitment while for higher positions promotion is the resort. Sound recruitment policy with the combination of methods could achieve good results.

Positive and Negative Recruitment- The wide dissemination about the recruitment for the best and most eligible candidate for appointment in government services is undertaken then it is called as positive method of recruitment whereas policy of exclusion is implemented to filter the undesirable and unfit based on narrower considerations then it is called as negative recruitment. In negative method of recruitment active role to attract the best is not performed. Normally when the number of applicants is much more than the available positions then the negative method is followed to exclude the unwanted.

Mass and Individual Recruitment- The large number of positions of generalist nature with no technical requirements are to be recruited then method of mass recruitment is adopted. The process of mass recruitment is tedious task involving examinations, interviews, etc. In individual method of recruitment the number of positions available is few and the nature of opening is technical, skill based requiring experience and specialization.

Recruitment Systems

Merit System- Today all the democracies in the world have adopted the merit based system of recruitment for the public services. The vacant posts in the government are filled by most deserving, competent, qualified individual selected through merit from open competition. Before the merit system was adopted there were three main systems followed in different parts of the world.

Sale of Offices- In *ancien régime* France i.e., before the Revolution of 1789 almost all posts of public responsibility had to be bought or inherited. French Kings sold privileged public offices it earned them more money than tax which further payments allowed them to sell or bequeath at will. By the eighteenth century, there were 70,000 venal offices, comprising the entire judiciary, most of the legal profession, officers in the army, and a wide range of other professions — from financiers handling the king's revenues down to auctioneers and even wigmakers. Though now yielding diminishing returns to the king, offices were more in demand than ever for the privileges and prestige, profit and power, that they conferred; and although it was widely accepted that selling public authority was undesirable, nobody imagined that those who had invested in offices could ever be bought out. The French Revolution brought an unexpected opportunity for this to happen, but the

22

legacy of venality has marked French institutions down to our day. This system was fundamental to the workings of state and society in France for over three centuries.[16]

Patronage System- The traditional view of the patronage system emphasizes its destabilizing political effects, holding it responsible for much of the factionalism and conflict disrupting early modern courts and governments. Competition for patronage created strife and hostility, and increased corruption, favoritism, and nepotism in government. These deleterious effects caused political instability. A newer, revisionist view, however, insists upon the constructive effects of patronage because it provided early modern governments with a powerful weapon of manipulation and control. The king and his ministers used the personal bonds of loyalty created by patronage to ensure that their decisions were carried out. They created their own patron-client networks or mobilized existing networks, and used them to enforce their policies. They distributed patronage to political opponents and unruly nobles to encourage their obedience, and withheld it to punish disobedience, thus reducing political strife and conflict. Philip II of Spain (ruled 1556–1598) his successor, Philip III (ruled 1598–1621), Elizabeth I of England (ruled 1558–1603) had four recognized favorites, the earls of Leicester and Essex, Sir Christopher Hatton, and Sir Walter Raleigh, but she always distributed patronage herself, and she skillfully played off court and government factions so that she was always in control. By the eighteenth century, however, power had shifted from the English crown to the Parliament, so it became the battleground for patronage, which was used to control parliamentary elections. Patronage allowed the government and the opposition to influence who sat in Parliament, and thus to determine what Parliament said and did. Cardinal Jules Mazarin (1602–1661), Louis XIV (ruled 1643–1715), Louis XIII (ruled 1610–1643), Cardinal Richelieu (1585–1642), The careers of Henry Howard, earl of Northampton (1540–1614), and Honoré d'Albert, sieur de Luynes, demonstrate the constructive uses of political patronage. Early modern governments used the selective distribution of patronage to enforce their policies and discipline unruly nobles. In this way, the patronage system helped to reduce strife and increase political stability.[17] Robert Walpole, regarded as the first prime minister of Great Britain also created a patronage system to reward his supporters with posts who used it as fief in an expanding and increasingly wealthy government. Patronage was criticized even by the Whig's who believed that politics had grown corrupt.

Spoils System- It was prevalent in USA during 1800's. The employees in the George Washington's administration were from Federalist Party towards which Washington has inclination. When Thomas Jefferson a democratic-republican came to power many of the federalists were dismissed and members of Democratic- Republican Party were given jobs. The credit to entrench the patronage or spoils system goes to President Andrew Jackson. He followed the policy of 'to the victor go the spoils' and brought 'Jacksonian Democrats' into office. He was of the opinion that the spoils system brings rotation in administration which is good for government. It was the assassination of President James Garfield in 1881 followed by the Pendleton Act brought spoils system to an end.

All the above discussed recruitment system are now redundant and obsolete and merit system has been accepted as the rational method in contemporary times.

Methods of Testing Merit

The methods followed to test merit for recruitment includes

- Written examination
- Interview or oral examination
- Performance testing
- Educational qualification and work experience
- Physical Test
- Psychological Test

TRAINING

Meaning

The dictionary meaning of training is the process of learning the skills you need to do a particular job or activity. According to Dale S. Beach training is the organized procedure by which people learn knowledge and skill for a definite purpose.[18] To Flippo training is the act of increasing knowledge and skill of an employee for doing a particular job.[19] Training is to provide instructions in a particular art, profession or occupation. The Assheton committee laid down aims of civil service training by emphasizing need of training for cultivating vocational expertise to enable the civil servant to do his business with precision and clarity, a flexibility of outlook to enable him to adjust to the needs of new times, and a capacity to equip him not only for performing his current duties more efficiently but also fitting him for other duties and also laid stress on the need to develop resistance to the danger of the civil servant becoming mechanized by the machine. The committee also remarked that the civil service need to be more consciously directed towards still higher ideals and standards of service and this can only be done by planned and purposeful training... the service must be pervaded with a sense of its obligation to the citizens...we rate high the need for civil servants to acquire right attitude of consideration and sympathy towards the members of the public but would add that this attitude should be mutual.[20]

Training is the process of developing skills, habits, knowledge and aptitudes in employees for the purpose of increasing the effectiveness of the employees in their present government position as well as preparing the employees for future government positions.[21] Training is a mindful, purposeful and deliberate effort of imparting instructions about a job or profession to improve the skills, knowledge and effectiveness of the employees so they can be ready for new tasks and higher responsibilities.

Training in Developing Countries

Training is very important for administration of all the countries particularly for developing countries where the administration is called on to play vital role in National reconstruction and socio- economic development. The properly trained efficient administration can only accomplish the gigantic task of development in the developing countries. The developing countries are befitted with the adversities and it is so even in the area of trained man power. The institutional setup and resources for training in such countries is either absent or inadequate. The complex and multifarious nature of the problems and the functions that need to be addressed requires expertise and professionally trained personnel. The trends and transformation that this societies' undergoes are dynamic and for the same requires administration to be innovative and efficient so that the development programmes could be speedily implemented.

Importance of Training

Training is important for ever expanding role of administration that is increasingly becoming complex, complicated and specialized. This need could be catered only through trained, expert and professional administration. The contemporary and traditional university education that is available does not fit the bill. Training is now an integral part of the modern personnel management. The need for training is now universally recognized for efficient modern administration. Training prepares an employee for new, varied and higher administrative responsibilities. Performance expectations, working methods and techniques, required skills, new knowledge, contemporary technological advances, best practices are taught and made clear during training help keep employees update. The overall orientation, changing work goals, objectives and strategy that are made explicitly clear during training is very crucial for the performance of the employees and later for its evaluation as well. Training is continuous educational process, a lifelong learning.

Objectives

1) Training improves employee's efficiency, occupational skills, and knowledge about recent developments

2) Training provides to the new recruits orientation about the organization and its objectives and goals.

3) Training prepares employees for organizational change, to shoulder higher responsibilities, and to undertake new and diverse tasks.

4) Training is vital for employees to overcome deficiencies and improve their integrity, motivation and morale.

5) Training fosters a sense of community service, people orientation, belongingness and camaraderie in the employees.

6) Training broadens the vision and outlook of the employees.

Types of Training

There are different types of training practiced in different countries some of the important are

- Formal and Informal training
- Short term and long term training.
- Pre-entry and post entry training.
- Centralized and departmental training
- Skills training and background training
- Orientation training.

Formal and Informal Training

Formal training is officially sanctioned and recognized training diligently organized under the expert supervision and guidance. Formal training has a course schedule with lectures, seminars, workshops, group discussion, symposium, project work, assignments, report writing, etc. Formal training may lead to the award of a professional degree or a certificate on successful completion of training. Formal training could be pre entry or post entry training. Formal training is undertaken full time or part time. Formal training can be orientation training, refresher course, short term course and can be of general or special nature. Formal training has to achieve predetermined course objectives, course schedule, methodology adopted, and evaluation process. Formal training is a continuous process and is conducted at the appropriate stages of career life.

Whatever an individual learns and acquires during the course of the actual working in the organization and by experience without making any special efforts is called as informal training. Informal training does not require extra efforts of planning and organizing the training paraphernalia. Informal training is the traditional method and is a very hard way of learning that requires a lot of perseverance and tolerance. It is slow, ineffective and frustrating.

Short Term and Long Term Training

This type of training takes into consideration the training content, duration required for course completion, training objectives of government and the nature of service that employees belongs. Training undertaken for few weeks to two months is called as short term and training of six months to two years is called as long term training

Pre-Entry and Post Entry

Pre-entry training prepares prospective recruits for service. The institutes and classes that undertake coaching for administrative careers in government is called as pre-entry training. The 'intern' and 'apprentice' is also pre-entry training that provides exposure and knowledge about governmental working. USA and European countries follow pre-entry training policy now a days in India also few pre-entry openings are made available in some departments of government.

The training that is imparted to person after joining the service is called as post- entry training or in- service training. This training makes use of formal and informal methodologies of training and it is undertaken at all the service levels of government. It helps improve efficiency, competency, and performance of the employees.

Centralized and Departmental Training

The training when imparted by the central training agency of the government is called as centralized training. The training programme undertaken by the department and organized only for the departmental employees is called as departmental training

Skills Training and Background Training

Training when focused to improve skills and competencies of the employees in particular kind of work are called as skills training. The techniques, knowledge, procedure to be followed about the skill are taught in this type of training.

The training that provides back ground study for better understanding of the context or working environment is called as background training. It helps employee understand the contextual multiplicity by learning sociology, political science, economics, history, law, public administration, etc. It widens the horizon of the employee and makes them able to comprehend the dynamics.

Orientation Training

This training is the introduction of the organization to the new entrants. Orientation training is planned to provide brief about the organization composition and functions. It introduces them to the job environment and informs about their role in the organization.

Techniques of Training

Lecture Method- Lecture method is oral presentation undertaken to provide information about a particular subject. Lecture is a time tested method. However it is monotonous and passive. It does not involve the trainee in the process of learning. The modern form of lecture method takes into account writing on a chalk-board, exercises, class questions and discussions, or presentations. Now the lecture method makes use of multimedia presentations by using graphics, websites, etc

Syndicate Method- In syndicate method a topic relevant to training is assigned to group and trainees are supposed to study this topic in-depth under a trainer supervisor. It may be either problem solving or knowledge gathering.

Case Study Method- Case study method is detail study of a single person, group, event, community, decisions, periods, projects, policies, institutions, or other systems. In this method actual cases are narrated by persons having experience of dealing with cases then the trainees study them individually, followed by discussion under supervision of the trainer.

Incidence Method- In this method the factual problems of administration are shared with trainees who are then asked to write their solution for the problem. Further the solution provided by the trainee is discussed and the trainee has to justify the prescribed solution, whereas the others will search to find faults. This method is helpful for developing decision making ability.

Role Play and Management Games- In role play method recreation of actual field situation in the class room is undertaken then the trainees perform specific roles relating to their post and after the performance the group undertakes a session to discuss roles and behavior of each participant.

Management games are used for training in management skills and also for evaluation of the trainees. Management games include activities to help trainees learn how to deal with different work situations.

Sensitivity Training- Sensitivity training makes people realize their own prejudices and idiosyncrasies and make them sensitive to others. The objective of this training is to condition the attitudes of the trainees to suit organizational goals. It provides an opportunity to self analysis and self development. Training group or T-group, developed by National Training Labs, USA is often cited as an example of sensitivity training is now part of National Education Association are now merged with encounter group that were designed for people having isolation related problems and is now divided and splintered into specialized topics, seeking to promote sensitivity. In recent times sensitivity training is portrayed negatively particularly by G. Edward Griffin[22] and Penn and Teller.[23]

Civil Service Training

Post 1935 period is characterized by the progressive rationalization of the management and training becoming vital element of personnel system. One of the fallacies in the early thinking about training was that employees hired under a merit system were qualified, were already 'trained', therefore for their jobs. To superimpose in-service training on top of this was either wasteful 'boondoggling' or an evidence that the initial selection of personnel was inadequate. This was naïve and shortsighted view.[24]

In modern times the social and political scenario has undergone rapid transformation. The emergence of Modern welfare state has enormously widened the scope of governmental activities. The nature of administration is undergoing sea change with the advent of advances in information, communication and technology. All these development has made administration complex and complicated activity. To address this, need for civil service training is felt strongly now than ever before.

CAREER PLANNING AND DEVELOPMENT

Meaning

The term career is a field for or pursuit of consecutive progressive achievement especially in public, professional, or business life.[25] The general course or progression of one's working life or one's professional achievements.[26] Career means advancement. The term career connote different meanings, the traditional notion of career is vertical progression in hierarchy coupled with increase in responsibilities, status and salary. The contemporary career means scope to individual potentials, demanding prospect, important vocation, and functional autonomy. Career is tangible progression through objectively defined career stages. Career is series of positions occupied during lifetime of an individual.

Career planning is individualistic as it includes formulation of individual career objectives based on personal career goal determined by aptitudes, aspirations, attraction, performance, etc. It is personal goal setting about the career. Career planning is process by which one identifies the means to achieve the career objectives. It could assume sequential form and must be realistic for its realization.

Career development on other hand is efforts taken by the organization to help employees attain their personal career goals. It involves institutional mechanism, processes and activities for accomplishment of the personal career objectives. A successful career system should make organizational objectives and individual aspirations compatible. The steps in career planning and development include recruitment; promotion; and retention.

Objectives

- The objective is to make available adequate qualified and competent personnel for future.

- Diligently planned succession policy, on positive side it ensures smooth transition and negatively it can be perfectly explained by idiomatic expression of Sydney Smith, to avoid "square peg in a round hole."

- To ensure that top position is open for all employees.

- To provide scope for overall development of the employees.

- Employee satisfaction as per their capacity, needs and expectations. The harmonious blending of organizational goals and individual aspirations are crucial for employee satisfaction and organizational objectives.

- In order to attract and retain best talent, compensation plan, retirement benefits, and motivation factors should be adequate enough for employees to trust the very intentions of the organizations concern for the employee's future. Sound career planning and development is guard against any possible dislocation, discontinuity and turnover of human talent.

Classification of Career System

Career systems are classified according to their scope, entrance and orientation. They are mutually inclusive in nature.

Program and Organization Careers- Career system in which persons are recruited for a particular program like construction, railways, etc than it is called as program careers. It ensures occupational specialties normally undertaken where work demands special education, training and experience.

Career system that allows movement of employees among various programmes and departments or agencies of government is termed as organizational careers eligibility, job identification, transferability, salaries, and retirement benefits are significant issues in such type of career advancement. There are many occupations in the government that can ensure and encourage movement of personnel.

Closed and Open Careers- The careers system with low maximum age limit for entry into services and almost all the higher level positions are entirely filled by promotion is called as closed career system. This type of system is found in various countries of the world. In this system equal opportunity for advancement is assured only if the base of hierarchy gets the personnel thereby the higher ranks will remain only for those already in service. Closed system includes the provision for 'selection out', in which employee reaching at the intermediate or lower higher level of the hierarchy in the organization must be either up to the benchmark standard to qualify for promotion or if unable to qualify they will have to retire prematurely from the services. Closed career system is often termed as 'monolithic' and 'monasteric' career systems.

Open career system as the name suggests allows entry based on competition to the eligible and qualified into the services at any level and any position. Individuals serving the government can also avail this opportunity. Open career system instills new blood and ideas at middle and higher levels of organization making bureaucracy flexible and people centric.

Job-Oriented Careers and Rank-in-Corps- The careers of individuals derived from the jobs to be performed is called as job oriented career. It is fitting of an individual into job. In it individual's career is a chain of assignments undertaken and it cut across programmes, departments even occupations. What matter is that, the person has to deliver the job requirements. The classification is based on duties and responsibilities. It is logical corollary of systematic division of responsibilities and division of labor. It is interchangeably referred as job oriented or rank-in-job career system. This concept is of US and Canadian origin and used in their public and private administration.

Rank-in-Corps is individual centric. Job assignments, utilization, rank and recognition are seen in terms of individual and the corps he belongs. This system facilitates the matching of employee skills with job needs. In this group camaraderie is important than the person attributes like position and performance and hence it is used by O. Glenn Stahl as Rank-in-Corps instead commonly used term of Rank-in-Man.[27] The countries with European influence use Rank-in-Man system in their civil service.

Career Stages

The gradual transitions that occur over time in the work life of an individual are called as career stages. Career stages are periods in which individuals work life is characterized by distinctive needs, concerns, tasks, and activities.[28] Various models of career stages are suggested by scholars like Erikson[29], Hall[30], Huse and Cummings[31], Dalton, Thompson and Price.[32] The most commonly used career typology formulates four stage career model that includes Formative/Establishment stage on entry level in service; Development/Advancement stage early level of career;

Mature/Maintenance stage at the mid level career; and Decline/Withdrawal stage is retirement level of career. Some authors has used the flowering stages as metaphor to explain this four stage typology as budding, blossoming, full bloom, and withering stage.

PERFORMANCE APPRAISAL

Meaning

Performance appraisal is the process of evaluating the performance and qualifications of the employees in terms of the requirement of the job of which they are employed, for purposes of administration including placement, selection for promotion, providing financial rewards and other actions which require differential treatment among the members of a group as distinguished from actions affecting all members equally.[33] The primary purpose of performance appraisal is to help each man handle his current job better.[34] Performance appraisal is the process by which a manager or consultant examines and evaluates an employee's work behavior by comparing it with preset standards, documents the results of the comparison, and uses the results to provide feedback to the employee to show where improvements are needed and why.[35]

Performance appraisals are employed to determine who needs what training, and who will be promoted, demoted, retained, or fired.

Need and Importance

In democratic countries government is accountable to people and to have a rational personnel policy is vital for manpower requirements of the government. A sound performance appraisal system is the basis for promotion in such a system. The employees come to know about their performance and become more responsible, works hard and aspire for promotion. The clarity in organizational objectives, well defined role and responsibilities, man power planning and training, and attractive reward system are imperative for a good performance appraisal system.

Objectives

- Develop a performance standard
- Job evaluation
- Identify weakness to be overcome by training
- Feedback and Control
- Transfers, Promotion and demotion

Methods of Performance Appraisal

Production Records- The nature of various works makes it possible to measure in units of production. In this system employees production as per the set norms is judged. The quality and quantity are the major issues in this type of appraisal system.

Ratings- in this employee of same cadre are ranked in order of merit. It is very simple form of performance appraisal.

Man-to-Man Comparison- In this method every employee is compared with every other in the group, the ranking is determined by the number of times the employee is judged better than the other.

Graphic Rating Scale- This is most widely used technique. It consists of traits such as quality of work, attitudes, quantity of work, etc, and the rater has to describe the degree of merit by marking on the descriptive phrases like 'excellent', 'good', 'poor', that are mentioned in the scale. This method is objective and uses various degrees of parameters and traits for judging employees. The descriptive phrases used in this method can mean different to different people and deciding relative weight-age becomes difficult and there is no scope for validation are major disadvantages of this method.

Critical Incident Method- In this method the exceptional thing for good and bad in the employees working is recorded. Assessment of employee is made based on his response and ability to handle such situations.

Free Written or Narrative Reports- This are simple written reports submitted by the supervisor about the employee. They may be structured or open end report but cover aspects of performance to be evaluated.

Coaching Appraisal- This is continuous process of observation of employee's performance by the supervisor, a type of supervision. This rating method improves mutual understanding and performance of the employee.

Forced Distribution Method- In this employees rated are distributed along five point scale in which predetermined fixed percentage of employee's (i.e.10% for best, 20% for good,40% for average, 20% for poor, and 10% for poorest) are to be included. Based on the performance supervisor assigns 10% of employees in best, 20% in good,40% in average, 20% in poor, and remaining 10% in poorest scale category.

Forced Choice Rating Method- In this statement and responses denoting characteristics of the employee are provided. In this only one response correctly identifies the statement and this scoring key must be kept secret. This is an objective method used by top management only to reaffirm their judgment.

Group Appraisal- This is appraisal by supervisor and few others from the organization who knows the employee and can be his superiors, colleagues and even subordinates.

Nomination- In the nomination method the supervisor identify and nominate the best and poor performers. In this sometimes panel of judges are also appointed to seek extra information about the nominations.

Work Sample Test- In this employees have to appear for work related tests which is than evaluated.

Result Oriented Performance Appraisal- This is evaluation of the goals or targets accomplishment of the employee. The appraisal also takes into consideration the objectives of organization to judge the potentialities and merit of the employee.

Efficiency Rating- It is the classification of all jobs. Efficiency rating is the official record of the way in which employee is doing the work of job. It is rated as excellent, very good, good, fair and unsatisfactory. Efficiency rating is the mechanical evaluation of all the traits of human character and personality. There is scope for inspection and appeals in efficiency ratings.

Confidential Reports- In most of the governments' confidential reports are used for performance appraisal and relates to performance, ability, and character of the employee. There are reporting officers and superior authority as countersigning authorities on confidential report.

Other Methods-

- Behaviorally anchored rating scales [BARS]
- Behavioral observation scales [BOS]
- Cost accounting method.

Factors affecting performance appraisal

Performance appraisal is a human exercise and witness bounded rationality in its process. The problem of subjectivity affects the objectivity in performance appraisal. The factors affecting it are

- Value system of the superiors.

- The nature of work is varied and has presence of diverse elements. They are dynamic, static, status-centric, inter-personal, non-work psyche, conformity oriented, etc
- Group allegiance
- Level of achievement
- Past record and reputation
- Influential contacts.
- Social standing
- Influence of personality

PROMOTION

Meaning

The term 'Promote' is derived from old French *promoter* which means to advance (someone) to a higher grade or office, and from Latin *promotus*, past participle of *promovere* is to move forward, advance; cause to advance, push onward; bring to light, reveal, from *pro-* 'forward' + *movere* 'to move'. In general sense it means to further the growth or progress of (anything).[36] The Webster dictionaries define it as advancement; elevation in rank; preferment; the state of being raised in status. The compact oxford reference dictionary gives the meaning as activity that supports or encourages and the movement to a higher position or rank. Promotion is an appointment from a given position to a position of higher grade involving a change of duties to a more difficult type of work and greater responsibility accompanied by change of title and usually by increase in pay.[37] Promotion involves change in the status and position of the employee.

Significance

The virtues of labor and truthfulness are appreciated because of promotion. The sense of appreciation and scope to move is an attraction for the talented to aspire to join the government service. Promotion is essential to retain employees in the service. Promotion provides chance for advancement, progress and satisfaction for the employees. Promotion involves higher duties, increased responsibilities, more authority, and rise in status accompanied by increased salary.

Types of Promotions

- Lower grade to a higher grade promotion in the same class. Example from junior clerk to senior clerk.

- Promotion from lower group to a higher group. Example from group 'B' service to group 'A' service.

- Promotion from lower service to higher service. Example from state service to all India service.

Principles of Promotion

The administrative structure is hierarchical there is little space at the top and as one moves up the ladder more heads fall down. This unavoidable nature could be overcome by adopting the principles of promotion in alternatives or in combination.

- Principle of seniority
- Merit Principle
- Seniority cum merit principle

Principle of Seniority- Promotion by seniority depends on the length of service rendered in a position, scale or grade. The senior most employees working in the organization are first promoted for doing so seniority list is prepared and followed in organization. In the case of exactly same length of service the person elder in age is considered senior. This principle is very simple as it is based on length of service; objective because gives no scope to favor; socially acceptable as seniority is respected; and democratic as it provides chance to all employees. The drawbacks of this principle are that it not rational as length of service cannot substitute merit thereby adversely affecting the efficiency of the government service. Furthermore it should be remembered that seniority not necessarily always coincides with age.

Merit Principle- As per this principle promotion is given to the most meritorious, and competent persons. Higher positions come with greater responsibilities, more challenges, complex working and diverse work settings that demands hardworking and brilliant individual talents, taken care by this principle. Merit principle if followed for promotion, helps improve efficiency and effectiveness in administration. It fosters spirit of competition in employees to work hard. It is criticized that merit is complex to measure objectively. Experience, seniority, and service spent in organization by the employee are neglected by merit.

Seniority-cum-Merit Principle- This principle advocates promotion for the senior most amongst the selected meritorious individuals.

General Pattern of Promotions

1) At top level of hierarchy promotion is by merit

2) At middle level of hierarchy basis of promotion is seniority cum merit

3) At lower level of hierarchy basis of promotion is seniority, but exceptional merit is also promoted.

Methods of Testing Merit for Promotion

Written and Oral Examination- It is the objective method of assessment of merit that provides chance to every aspirant to compete for promotion. In this there is no scope for favoritism and discrimination. This method proves to be an opportunity for the deserving and brilliant employees. This method adversely affects the working as employees concentrate on examinations instead of doing their jobs. The senior and experienced employees find it difficult to study and memorize for examinations.

Efficiency Ratings- Efficiency rating is carried on the basis of service record by judging the employees against various traits and parameters. The employees are rated as excellent, very good, good, fair and unsatisfactory. The process is subjective and based on the opinion of the superior whose whims, idiosyncrasies and value setting adversely affects the rating. It is difficult to evolve it as a rational for testing merit for promotion.

Personal Judgment of the Head- Personal judgment of the head decides merit leaving ample chance for authoritarian tendencies to promote 'yesmanship' and 'sycophancy'. It is depressing for sincere and sensitive employees.

Essentials of Proper Promotion System

According to W.F. Willoughby essentials of sound promotion system are[38]

- Adoption of standard specifications setting forth the duties and qualifications required for all promotions in the government service.

- The classification of these positions into distinct classes, series, grades and services

- The inclusion of all positions except those of a policy making (political) character into this classification

- The adoption so far as possible of the principles of recruitment from within for filling up of higher posts

- The adoption of the principle of merit in determining the selection of employees for promotion

- The provision for adequate means for determining the relative merit of employees eligible for promotion

PAY AND SERVICE CONDITION

Introduction

Civil Service is the most coveted career choice of the bright and talented aspirants. The members earn their living by serving in it. Pay is money due for work. The pay scales are vital elements of status in the belief of public. Pay constitutes the most important single factor among the attractions of government service. It is the main source of motivation and very dear sensitive issue for employees.

Methods of Pay Fixation

The method of pay fixation depends on various system of administration that country follows. Some of the important methods are

- Salaries are fixed by Legislation.
- Broad salary framework by legislature and details by delegated legislation (executive).
- Salaries fixed by collective bargaining in private employment even in public undertakings.
- Salaries fixed by local boards
- No planned system

Job Evaluation

The performance of any job demands certain skills, education, experience, work condition, etc. Pay for work takes into consideration all this. Job evaluation is a method of deciding the value or worth of a job as compared to other jobs in an organization. It undertakes comparative assessment to decide the relative worth or value on which pay structure is formulated that provides for pay according to worth. Job evaluation is the method to determine pay structure. The important methods of job evaluation are

- Ranking method
- Classification method (Grading method)
- Factor comparison method or Point method
- Market Pricing

The above two are non-quantitative and last two are quantitative method.

Principles of Pay Fixation

The pay scales of government employees are fixed by making following considerations.

- Pays should be compatible with private employment. There should be fair relativity between pay of government and private employment. Pay should not be less favorable to private but more so if possible.

- State as model employer postulates that state as an employer in matter of service conditions and pay should be ahead of other employers.

- Employer should pay what is necessary to recruit and retain an efficient staff. Factors of responsibility, cost of living, marriage, children, social position, etc, are assumed in it.[39]

- The pay should be commensurate with the cost of living

- Pay structure should be related to the resources and the per capita income of the country. Pay should be just, equitable and follow equal pay for equal work.

In this regard the evidence of the controller of the establishment department of the British treasury before the Tomlin commission is succinct.

The principle on which successive governments have acted in regard to the remuneration of the civil service might... be summarized as follows:

The first principle is that remuneration is only one of a number of factors in the conditions of service of civil servants and that in fixing remuneration due regard must be had to those other factors in the conditions of employment of civil servants, notably security of tenure, prospects of promotion, leave and sick leave privileges, and pensionability.

Subject to that it has been held essential that the remuneration and other conditions of employments of civil servants shall be adequate to ensure the recruitment to the civil service of a fully qualified staff, and the maintenance of an efficient and healthy civil service.

It has followed from this principle that the rates of remuneration and other conditions of employment in the public service must be such as to compare well with the rates of remuneration and other conditions of service normally available outside the service in competing occupations.

Beyond that it has been held that to achieve the main object to which I have referred...it would not be right to prescribe for civil servants rates of remuneration and conditions of service which were out of scale with the standards normally obtaining amongst good employers outside the public service...they must not...on this comparison be too low; nor...ought they to be unduly high, because any such disparity...would have the effect of elevating civil servants into a privileged class and so of doing an injustice to the community which 'ex hypothesi' would be worse off, and has always to foot the bill.

More than that, it has been held... that the remuneration of civil servants should, as far as possible, be so fixed as to endure for a considerable period of time. The result is that the remuneration of the civil service is apt to fluctuate less from ear to year than the remuneration in... outside industry where the terms of the employment for the staff are subject to more or less frequent variations according as...industry is faring well or ill.[40]

The Policy of the Government

The political milieu, ideology of government, tone of opposition determines pay fixation policy of the government. The broad motive is to attract new and to promote and retain existing employees.

The job evaluation, rating techniques and compensation plan should be separate, distinct, flexible, responsive, relevant, methodological, and clear. The features incorporated in the plan should be consistent with organization objectives, rational and in public interest.

Service Condition

Service conditions are vital for effective and efficient working of the employees in the organizations. Apart from salary it encompasses all other tangible and intangible conditions of employments.

Leave- Time allowed away from work for holiday, rest or for private business. The types of leave include earned leave or privilege leave, sick leave, study leave, casual leave, and leave without pay.

Holidays- A holiday is a day set aside by employer, custom or law on which work is suspended. Holidays can be weekly, and on days of local, national and religious importance

Hours of work- Working hours are determined by employer, rules or law and cannot be same for all the departments

Office Accommodation and Staff welfare- The workplace environment both positively and negatively impacts employee morale, motivation, performance and engagement.

Negotiation Machinery- For grievance redressal by participation of public servants in negotiating and rendering advice to the government and settling, disputes in the public service and to provide for related matters.

Incentives- It is something additional to the normal salary that motivates employee for action. It may be in the form of remunerative, financial, moral, coercive and natural incentive.

Compensation- Compensation is awarded in recognition of loss suffering and injury. It can be in cash or kind.

Allowances and Perks- The allowances are

- Dearness allowance- to compensate the employees for inflation
- City compensatory allowance - City travel
- House rent allowance- To cover house rent facility account to basic pay.
- Traveling Allowance- Expenses incur on traveling on official work.
- Daily Allowance- Maintenance charges to employee for each day of absence from head quarter for official work.

- Leave travel concession- Welfare measure.

- Medical Allowance - Welfare measure

- Conveyance Allowance - Transportation of luggage from one place to another.

- Uniform Allowance

- Children Education allowance

RETIREMENT BENEFITS

Introduction

Employees can work up to certain age in efficient and effective manner. Every employment has a prescribed age of retirement. Old age brings in limitation on the functioning of persons. Retirement provides scope for new blood to enter in the organization and also provides for retirement benefits to the employees who have served the best part of their life for the organization to take care of their needs for the rest of life. A retirement system for civil employees is primarily designed to facilitate the termination of employment of men and women whose powers have failed on account of age or disability by granting allowance for past services, to provide benefits to dependants in case of death and to improve the morale of the services by creating a sense of economic security. From the point of view of the employee, the retirement system helps to compensate for modest scale of pay, relieves anxiety for the future and furnishes a convenient means of regular saving.[41] The retirement benefits provide financial security and stability during old age to employees when they don't have a regular income source. Retirement benefits ensure that employees live with dignity and without compromising on their standard of living during the latter part of their life. According to United

60

Nations Population Division World's life expectancy is expected to reach 75 years by 2050 from present level of 65 years. The better health and sanitation conditions in India have increased the life span. As a result number of post-retirement years increases. Thus, rising cost of living, inflation and life expectancy make retirement planning essential part of today's life.[42] Government provides social security to its employees.

Aims and Objectives of Retirement

- To provide permanence to public services
- It aims at increasing the efficiency
- Helps maintain system of promotion
- To allow young people to join civil services
- Satisfaction and security for employees
- Role of State as ideal employer

Main Features of Retirement System

- Retirement is compulsory at fixed age by taking into consideration the nature of the work, demographic factors, effective working life, and other factors.
- Retirement system gives pension to the retired employees but cannot be claimed by them as a right and can be withdrawn by government in financial contingency.
- The benefits of General Provident Fund, group life insurance schemes, etc can be derived at the time of retirement by the government employees.

Classes of Pension

In India the classes of pensions available are[43]

Superannuation- A superannuation pension shall be granted to a Government servant who is retired on his attaining the age of 60 years.

Retiring Pension-A retiring pension shall be granted to a Government servant who retires, or is retired before attaining the age of Superannuation or to a Government servant who, on being declared surplus opts, for voluntary retirement.

Voluntary Retirement- Any Government servant can apply for voluntary retirement, three months in advance, only after the completion of twenty years of his qualifying service, provided there is no vigilance or Departmental Enquiry pending /initiated against him/her.

Invalid Pension- Invalid Pension may be granted if a Government servant applies for retirement from the service on account of any bodily or mental infirmity which permanently incapacitates him/her for the service. The request for invalid pension has to be supported by medical report from the competent medical board.

Compensation Pension- If a Government servant is selected for discharge owing to the abolition of a permanent post, he shall, unless he is appointed to another post the conditions of which are deemed by the authority competent to discharge him/her to be at least equal to those of his own, have the option (a) of taking compensation pension to which he may be entitled for the service he had rendered, or

(b) of accepting another appointment on such pay as may be offered and continuing to count his previous service for pension.

Compulsory Retirement Pension- A Government servant compulsorily retired from service as a penalty may be granted, by the authority competent to impose such penalty, pension or gratuity, or both at a rate not less than two-thirds and not more than full compensation pension or gratuity, or both admissible to him on the date of his compulsory retirement. The pension granted or allowed shall not be less than Rs. 3500/- p.m.

Compassionate Allowance- (i) A Government servant who is dismissed or removed from service shall forfeit his pension and gratuity:

Provided that the authority competent to dismiss or remove him from service may, if the case is deserving of special consideration, sanction a compassionate allowance not exceeding two-thirds of pension or gratuity or both which would have been admissible to him if he had retired on compensation pension.

(ii) A compassionate allowance sanctioned under the proviso to sub-rule (i) shall not be less than the amount of Rupees one thousand nine hundred and thirteen per mensem.

Extraordinary Pension- Extraordinary Pension in the form of Disability pension/extraordinary family pension may be paid to the Government servant/his family if disablement/death (or the aggravation of disablement/death) of the Government servant, during his service, are attributed to the Government service. For the award of extraordinary pension, there should thus be a casual connection between disablement and Government service; and death and Government service, for attributability or aggravation to be conceded. The quantum of the pension, however, depends upon the category of the disablement/death.

Government servants appointed on or after 1.1.2004 are not covered by the CCS (Extraordinary Pension) Rules.

Family Pension- Family pension is granted to the widow / widower and where there is no widow / widower to the children of a Government servant who entered in service in a pensionable establishment on or after 01/01/1964 but on or before 31.12.2003 or having entered service prior to that date came to be governed by the provisions of the Family Pension Scheme for Central Government Employees, 1964 if such a Government servant-

(i) dies while in service on or after 01/01/1964 or

(ii) retired/died before 31.12.1963 or

(iii) retires on or after 01/01/1964

and at the time of his death was in receipt of pension.

Family pension is payable to the children up to 25 years of their age, or marriage or till they start earning a monthly income exceeding Rs.3,500/- + DA admissible from time to time p.m. whichever is earlier.

Widow daughter / divorced daughter/ unmarried daughter of deceased Government servant is also entitled for the family pension till her remarriage or up to life time or starts earning a monthly income exceeding Rs.3,500/- + DA admissible from time to time p.m. whichever is earlier.

Family pension is also payable to the dependent parents of deceased Government servants w.e.f. 01/01/98, where there is no claimant i.e. spouse or child for family pension, alive.

If the son or daughter, of a Government servant is suffering from any disorder or disability of mind or is physically crippled or disabled so as to render him or her unable to earn a living even after attaining the age of 25 years, the family pension can continue to be paid for life time subject to conditions.

Retirement benefits in India

The government of India employee is entitled for the following retirement benefits[44]

Pension- The minimum eligibility period for receipt of pension is 10 years. A Government servant retiring in accordance with the Pension Rules is entitled to receive superannuation pension on completion of at least 10 years of qualifying service.

In the case of Family Pension the widow is eligible to receive pension on death of her spouse after completion of one year of continuous service or before even completion of one year if the Government servant had been examined by the appropriate Medical Authority and declared fit for Government service. It is with effect from 1.1.2006, Pension is calculated with reference to average emoluments namely, the average of the basic pay drawn during the last 10 months of the service or last basic pay drawn whichever is beneficial. Full pension with 10/20 years of qualifying service is 50% of the average emoluments or last basic pay drawn whichever is beneficial. Before 1.1.2006, for qualifying service of less than 33 years, amount of pension was proportionate to the actual qualifying service broken into completed half-year periods. For example, if total qualifying service is 30 years and 4 months (i.e. 61 half-year periods), pension will be calculated as under:-

Pension amount = R/2(X) 61/66 where R represents average reckonable emoluments for last 10 months of qualifying service or the last pay drawn as opted by the government servant.

Minimum pension presently is Rs. 3500 per month. Maximum limit on pension is 50% of the highest pay in the Government of India (presently Rs. 45,000) per month. Pension is payable up to and including the date of death.

Commutation of Pension

A Government servant has an option to commute a portion of pension, not exceeding 40% of it, into a lump sum payment with effect from 1.1.1996. No medical examination is required if the option is exercised within one year of retirement. If the option is exercised after expiry of one year, he/she will have to undergo medical examination by the specified competent authority.

Lump sum payable is calculated with reference to the Commutation Table constructed on an actuarial basis. The monthly pension will stand reduced by the portion commuted and the commuted portion will be restored on the expiry of 15 years from the date of receipt of the commuted value of pension. Dearness Relief, however, will continue to be calculated on the basis of the original pension (i.e. without reduction of commuted portion).

The formula for arriving for commuted value of Pension (CVP) is

CVP = 40 % (X) Commutation factor* (X) 12

* The commutation factor will be with reference to age next birthday on the date on which commutation becomes absolute as per the New Table as Annexure to this Departments O.M. No. 38/37/08- P&PW(A) dated 2.9.2008

Retirement and Death Gratuity- This is payable to the retiring Government servant. A minimum of 5 years qualifying service and eligibility to receive service gratuity/pension is essential to get this one time lump sum benefit. Retirement gratuity is calculated @ 1/4th of a month's Basic Pay plus Dearness Allowance drawn before retirement for each completed six monthly period of qualifying service. There is no minimum limit for the amount of gratuity. The retirement gratuity payable is 16 times the Basic Pay, subject to a maximum of Rs. 10 lakhs.

Death Gratuity is a one-time lump sum benefit payable to the widow/widower or the nominee of a permanent or a quasi-permanent or a temporary Government servant, including CPF beneficiaries, dying in harness. There is no stipulation in regard to any minimum length of service rendered by the deceased employee. Entitlement of death gratuity is regulated as

Qualifying Service	Rate
Less than one year	2 times of basic pay
One year or more but less than 5 years	6 times of basic pay
5 years or more but less than 20 years	12 times of basic pay
20 years of more	Half of emoluments for every completed 6 monthly period of qualifying service subject to a maximum of 33 times of emoluments.

Maximum amount of Death Gratuity admissible is Rs. 10 lakhs w.e.f. 1.1.2006

Service Gratuity- A retiring Government servant will be entitled to receive service gratuity (and not pension) if total qualifying service is less than 10 years. Admissible amount is half month's basic pay last drawn for each completed 6 monthly period of qualifying service. There is no minimum or maximum monetary limit on the quantum. This one time lump sum payment is distinct from and is paid over and above the retirement gratuity.

Issue of No Demand Certificate- Dues owed by the retiring employees on account of License Fee for Government accommodation, advances, over payment of pay and allowances are required to be assessed by the Head of Office and intimated to the Accounts Officer two months in advance of the date of retirement so that these are recovered from retirement gratuity before payment. For this purpose the License Fee for those in occupation of Government accommodation is taken into account up to the end of the permissible period for which accommodation can be retained after retirement under the Rules on normal rent. The recovery of License Fee beyond that period is the responsibility of the Directorate of Estates. If, for any reason final dues cannot be assessed on time, then 10% of gratuity is withheld from gratuity

General Provident Fund and Incentives- As per General Provident Fund (Central Services) Rules, 1960, all temporary Government servants after a continuous service of one year, all re-employed pensioners (Other than those eligible for admission to the Contributory Provident Fund) and all permanent Government servants are eligible to subscribe to the Fund. A subscriber, at the time of joining the fund is required to make a nomination, in the prescribed form, conferring on one or more persons the right to receive the amount that may stand to his credit in the fund in the event of his death, before that amount has become payable or having become payable has not been paid. A subscriber shall subscribe monthly to the Fund except during the period when he is under suspension. Subscriptions to the Provident Fund are stopped 3 months prior to the date of superannuation. Rates of subscription shall not be less than 6% of subscriber's emoluments and not more than his total emoluments. Rate of interest on GPF accumulations with effect from 1.4.2009 is 8% compounded annually and the rate of interest will vary according to notifications of the Government. The Rules provide for drawal of advances/ withdrawals from the Fund for specific purposes.

Deposit Linked Insurance Revised Scheme- Under the GPF Rules, on the death of subscriber, the person entitled to receive the amount standing to the credit of the subscriber shall be paid an additional amount equal to the average balance in the account during the 3 years immediately preceding the death of the subscriber subject to certain conditions provided in the relevant Rule. The additional amount payable under that Rule shall not exceed Rs. 60,000/-. To get this benefit, the subscriber should have put in at least 5 years service at the time of his/her death.

Contributory Provident Fund- The Contributory Provident Fund Rules (India), 1962 are applicable to every non-pensionable servant of the Government belonging to any of the services under the control of the President. A subscriber, at the time of joining the Fund is required to make a nomination in the prescribed Form conferring on one or more persons the right to receive the amount that may stand to his credit in the

Fund in the event of his death, before that amount has become payable or having become payable has not been paid.

A subscriber shall subscribe monthly to the Fund when on duty or Foreign Service but not during the period of suspension. Rates of subscription shall not be less than 10% of the emoluments and not more than his emoluments. The employer's contribution at that percentage prescribed by the Government will be credited to the subscriber's account and this is 10%. Rate of interest with effect from 1.4.2009 is 8% compounded annually. The Rules provide for drawal of advances/ withdrawals from the CPF for specific purposes. As in GPF Rules, the CPF Rules also provide for Deposit Linked Insurance Revised Scheme.

Leave Encashment- Encashment of leave is a benefit granted under the CCS (Leave) Rules and not a pensionary benefit. Encashment of Earned Leave/Half Pay Leave standing at the credit of the retiring Government servant is admissible on the date of retirement subject to a maximum of 300 days. There is no provision under the Rule for payment of interest on delayed payment of Leave Encashment.

Group Insurance Scheme- A portion of monthly contributions paid while in service is credited in a Saving Fund, on which interest accrues. A Government servant while entering service has to apply in Form No. 4 of the above

Scheme to the Head of Office, who shall issue a sanction for the payment of subscriber's accumulation in the Savings Fund segment together with interest and arrange for its disbursement, soon after retirement. Payments under this Scheme are made in accordance with the Table of Benefit which takes in to account interest up to the date of cessation of service. Insurance cover benefit under this Scheme is available to the family in the event of death of the subscriber. No interest is payable on account of delayed payments under this Scheme.

Travelling Allowance on Retirement- The Government servant shall, besides the fares are also eligible to composite transfer grant equal to one month's basic pay, if the distance from the last station of duty is more than 20 km.

Pension Fund Regulatory and Development Authority

The Pension Fund Regulatory and Development Authority Act, was passed on 19th September, 2013 and the same was notified on 1st February, 2014. PFRDA is regulating National Pension System, subscribed by employees of Government of India, State Governments and by employees of private institutions, organizations and unorganized sectors.[45]

National Pension System[46]

Retirement planning involves disciplined saving, vigilant investment to build a sufficient retirement corpus and its judicious drawdown in the post-retirement phase. This is achieved by joining a pension/retirement plan at an early stage in one's life so that when a person retires from active work life, gets a regular stream of income in the form of pension or annuity for his life. The Central Government has introduced the Defined Contribution based Pension System known as the National Pension System (NPS) replacing the existing system of Defined Benefit Pension with effect from January 01, 2004. Many State Governments have adopted NPS architecture and implemented NPS mandatorily through Gazette Notifications for their employees joining on or after a cut-off date.

NPS is a voluntary, defined contribution retirement savings scheme designed to enable the subscribers to make optimum decisions regarding their future through systematic savings during their working life. NPS seeks to inculcate the habit of saving for retirement amongst the citizens. It is an attempt towards finding a sustainable solution to the problem of providing adequate retirement income to every citizen of India. Under the NPS, individual savings are pooled in to a pension fund which are invested by PFRDA regulated professional fund managers as per the approved investment guidelines in to the diversified portfolios comprising of government bonds, bills, corporate debentures and shares. These contributions would grow and accumulate over the years, depending on the returns earned on the investment made. At the time of normal exit from NPS, the subscribers may use the accumulated pension wealth under the scheme to purchase a life annuity from a PFRDA empanelled life insurance company apart from withdrawing a part of the accumulated pension wealth as lump-sum, if they choose so. NPS offers a range of investment options and choice of Pension Fund Manager for planning the growth of employee's investments in a reasonable manner and see their money grow. Individuals can switch over from one investment option to another or from one fund manager to another subject, of course, to certain regulatory restrictions. The returns are totally market-related. Simple – Opening an account with NPS provides a Permanent Retirement Account Number, which is a unique number and it remains with the subscriber throughout his lifetime. The scheme is structured into two tiers:

Tier-I account: This is the non-withdrawable permanent retirement account into which the accumulations are deposited and invested as per the option of the subscriber.

Tier-II account: This is a voluntary withdrawable account which is allowed only when there is an active Tier I account in the name of the subscriber. The withdrawals are permitted from this account as per the needs of the subscriber as and when claimed.

NPS provides seamless portability across jobs and across locations, unlike all current pension plans, including that of the employee provident fund. It would provide hassle-free arrangement for the individual subscribers.

Besides the NPS, some mutual funds and insurance companies also offer Pension plan or retirement plan, which are not under the jurisdiction of PFRDA. Apart from this the normal retirement plan options include employee provident fund, retirement gratuity etc. is offered by employers to their workers and employees.

DISCIPLINE

Meaning

Merriam-Webster's Learner's Dictionary defines discipline as control that is gained by requiring that rules or orders be obeyed and punishing bad behavior; a way of behaving that shows a willingness to obey rules or orders; and behavior that is judged by how well it follows a set of rules or orders.[47] Discipline is the training that makes people more willing to obey or more able to control themselves, often in the form of rules, and punishments if these are broken, or the behaviour produced by this training.[48] Retirement benefits, salary, promotion, incentives are definitely good efforts of personnel system to have effectiveness and efficiency in the organizations, but this is not enough for the same. Human nature is not always virtuous but to keep it so personnel system needs discipline and code of conduct. One must accept the fact that the uncorrectable bad performance and intolerable misconduct do in actuality occur. No organization is so perfect, no executive so ingenious, no personnel system so infallible that measures of correction and punishment can be completely avoided.[49] According to Spriegel, Discipline is a force that prompts an individual or a group to observe the rules regulations and procedure which are deemed to be necessary to the attainment of an objective it is force or fear of an objective it is force or fear of force which restrains an individual or a group from doing things which are deemed to be destructive of group objectives. It is also the exercise of restraint or the enforcement of the penalties for the violation of group regulations.[50] Disciplinary action is an administrative way to correct the misconduct of the employee. The purpose may be reformatory, deterrent or retributory.

Offences by Public Servants

Indian Penal Code- Chapter IX of Indian Penal Code, 1861 deals with offences by or relating to public servants, they are

Section 161 to 165A- Repealed by the Prevention of Corruption Act, 1988 (49 of 1988), s. 31.

Section 166- Public servant disobeying law, with intent to cause injury to any person

Section 166A- Public Servant disobeying direction under Law [vide Criminal Law (Amendment) Act, 2013]

Section 166B- Punishment for non treatment of victim [vide Criminal Law (Amendment) Act, 2013]

Section 167- Public servant framing an incorrect document with intent to cause injury

Section 168- Public servant unlawfully engaging in trade

Section 169- Public servant unlawfully buying or bidding for property

The Prevention of Corruption Act, 1988- The chapter III of this act deals with the offences and penalties they are

Section 7- Public servant taking gratification other than legal remuneration in respect of an official act

Section 8- Taking gratification, in order, by corrupt or illegal means, to influence public servant

Section 9- Taking gratification, for exercise of personal influence with public servant

Section 10- Punishment for abetment by public servant of offences defined in section 8 or 9

Section 11- Public servant obtaining valuable thing, without consideration from person concerned in proceeding or business transacted by such public servant

Section 12- Punishment for abetment of offences defined in section 7 or 11

Whoever abets any offence punishable under section 7 or section 11 whether or not that offence is committed in consequence of that abetment, shall be punishable with imprisonment for a term which shall be not less than six months but which may extend to five years and shall also be liable to fine,

Section 13- Criminal misconduct by a public servant

(1) A public servant is said to commit the offence of criminal misconduct,-

(a) if he habitually accepts or obtains or agrees to accept or attempts to obtain from any person for himself or for any other person any gratification other than legal remuneration as a motive or reward such as is mentioned in section 7; or

(b) if he habitually accepts or obtains or agrees to accept or attempts to obtain for himself or for any other person, any valuable thing without consideration or for a consideration which he knows to be inadequate from any person whom he knows to have been, or to be, or to be likely to be concerned in any proceeding or business transacted or about to be transacted by him, or having any connection with the official functions of himself or of any public servant to whom he is subordinate, or from any person whom he knows to be interested in or related to the person so concerned; or

(c) if he dishonestly or fraudulently misappropriates or otherwise converts for his own use any property entrusted to him or under his control as a public servant or allows any other person so to do; or

(d) if he,-

(i) by corrupt or illegal means, obtains for himself or for any other person any valuable thing or pecuniary advantage; or

(ii) by abusing his position as a public servant, obtains for himself or for any other person any valuable thing or pecuniary advantage; or

(iii) while holding office as a public servant, obtains for any person any valuable thing or pecuniary advantage without any public interest; or

(e) if he or any person on his behalf, is in possession or has, at any time during the period of his office, been in possession for which the public servant cannot satisfactorily account, of pecuniary resources or property disproportionate to his known sources of income.

Explanation.-For the purposes of this section, "known sources of income" means income received from any lawful source and such receipt has been intimated in accordance with the provisions of any law, rules or orders for the time being applicable to a public servant.

(2) Any public servant who commits criminal misconduct shall be punishable with imprisonment for a term which shall be not less than one year but which may extend to seven years and shall also be liable to fine.

Section 14- Habitual committing of offence under sections 8, 9 and 12

Whoever habitually commits-

(a) an offence punishable under section 8 or section 9; or

(b) an offence punishable under section 12,

shall be punishable with imprisonment for a term which shall be not less than two years but which may extend to seven years and shall also be liable to fine.

Section 15- Punishment for attempt

Whoever attempts to commit an offence referred to in clause (c) or clause (d) of sub-section (1) of section 13 shall be punishable with imprisonment for a term which may extend to three years and with fine.

16. Matters to be taken into consideration for fixing fine

Where a sentence of fine is imposed. under sub-section (2) of section 13 or section 14, the court in fixing the amount of the fine shall taken into consideration the amount or the value of the property, if any, which the accused person has obtained by committing the offence or where the conviction is for an offence referred to in clause (e) of sub-section (1) of section 13, the pecuniary resources or property referred to in that clause for which the accused person is unable to account satisfactorily.

The disciplinary proceedings are initiated as per the appropriate laws and rules for misconduct and misdemeanor, they are

Cases of Misconduct

   1. Embezzlement
   2. Falsification of accounts not amounting to misappropriation of money

3.Fraudulent claims

4.Forgery of documents, theft of government property

5.Defrauding government, bribery, corruption

6.Possession of disproportionate asserts

7.Offences against law applicable to government servant

Conduct Amounting to Misdemeanor

1.Disobedience of order

2.Insubordination

3.Misbehavior - Superior / Colleagues / Subordinate / members of public

4.Misconduct – Violation of conduct rules / standing orders and insolvency/ intrigues and conspiracy.

Types of Disciplinary Action

- Informal
- Formal

Informal Disciplinary Action- It includes

1.Assignment to a less desirable work

2.Close supervision

3.Loss or withholding of privileges

4.Failure of consultation in relevant matters

5.Rejection of proposals or recommendation

6.Curtailing authority and diminishing responsibility.

7.Withholding of increment of pay

8.Recovery from pay

Formal Disciplinary Action- The formal disciplinary action is undertaken where the offences are of serious nature and can be established legally. The All India Services (Discipline and Appeal) Rules, 1969, Civil Services (Classification, Control and Appeal) Rules, 1965, Part V, deals with the penalties for good and sufficient reasons imposed on a Government servant are as under

Minor Penalties

i   censure;

ii   withholding of promotion;

iii   recovery from pay of the whole or part of any pecuniary loss caused by him to the Government by negligence or breach of orders;

iii a   reduction to a lower stage in the time-scale of pay by one stage for a period not exceeding three years, without cumulative effect and not adversely affecting his pension; and

iv   withholding of increments of pay

Major Penalties

v.   save as provided for in clause (iii) (a), reduction to a lower stage in the time-scale of pay for a specified period, with further directions as to whether or not the Government servant will earn increments of pay during the period of such reduction and whether on the expiry of such period, the reduction will or will not have the effect of postponing the future increments of his pay

vi.   reduction to lower time-scale of pay, grade, post or Service for a period to be specified in the order of penalty, which shall be a bar to the promotion of the Government servant during such specified period to the time-scale of pay, grade, post or service from which he was reduced, with direction as to whether or not, on promotion on the expiry of the said specified period -

(a) the period of reduction to time-scale of pay, grade, post or service shall operate to postpone future increments of his pay, and if so, to what extent; and

(b) the Government servant shall regain his original seniority in the higher time scale of pay , grade, post or service;

vii.   compulsory retirement;

viii.   removal from service which shall not be a disqualification for future employment under the Government;

ix.   dismissal from service which shall ordinarily be a disqualification for future employment under the Government.

Provided that, in every case in which the charge of possession of assets disproportionate to known-source of income or the charge of acceptance from any person of any gratification, other than legal remuneration, as a motive or reward for doing or forbearing to do any official act is established, the penalty mentioned in clause (viii) or clause (ix) shall be imposed.

Provided further that in any exceptional case and for special reasons recorded in writing, any other penalty may be imposed.

Explanation- The following shall not amount to a penalty within the meaning of this rule, namely

i. withholding of increments of a Government servant for his failure to pass any departmental examination in accordance with the rules or orders governing the Service to which he belongs or post which he holds or the terms of his appointment;

ii. stoppage of a Government servant at the efficiency bar in the time-scale of pay on the ground of his unfitness to cross the bar;

iii. non-promotion of a Government servant, whether in a substantive or officiating capacity, after consideration of his case, to a Service, grade or post for promotion to which he is eligible;

iv. reversion of a Government servant officiating in a higher Service, grade or post to a lower Service, grade or post, on the ground that he is considered to be unsuitable for such higher Service, grade or post or on any administrative ground unconnected with his conduct;

v. reversion of a Government servant, appointed on probation to any other Service, grade or post, to his permanent Service, grade or post during or at the end of the period of probation in accordance with the terms of his appointment or the rules and orders governing such probation;

vi. replacement of the services of a Government servant, whose services had been borrowed from a State Government or any authority under the control of a State Government, at the disposal of the State Government or the authority from which the services of such Government servant had been borrowed;

vii. compulsory retirement of a Government servant in accordance with the provisions relating to his superannuation or retirement;

viii.   termination of the services -

a) of a Government servant appointed on probation, during or at the end of the period of probation, in accordance with the terms of appointment or the rules and orders governing such probation

Mode of Taking Disciplinary Action

The power to take disciplinary action should be vested in the authority having power to appoint. The President of India is the disciplinary authority in respect of All India Services, Central Services Group 'A' and some Group 'B' services. The Secretary of the concerned Ministry is the disciplinary authority in respect of Group 'C' and 'D' employees.

Articles of Indian Constitution Dealing with Disciplinary Matters

Article 309- Recruitment and conditions of service of persons serving the Union or a State Subject to the provisions of this Constitution, Acts of the appropriate Legislature may regulate the recruitment, and conditions of service of persons appointed, to public services and posts in connection with the affairs of the Union or of any State: Provided that it shall be competent for the President or such person as he may direct in the case of services and posts in connection with the affairs of the Union, and for the Governor of a State or such person as he may direct in the case of services and posts in connection with the affairs of the State, to make rules regulating the recruitment, and the conditions of service of persons appointed, to such services and posts until provision in that behalf is made by or under an Act of the appropriate Legislature under this article, and any rules so made shall have effect subject to the provisions of any such Act

Article 310- Tenure of office of persons serving the Union or a State

(1) Except as expressly provided by this Constitution, every person who is a member of a defence service or of a civil service of the Union or of an all India service or holds any post connected with defence or any civil post under the Union, holds office during the pleasure of the President, and every person who is a member of a civil service of a State or holds any civil post under a State holds office during the pleasure of the Governor of the State

(2) Notwithstanding that a person holding a civil post under the Union or a State holds office during the pleasure of the President or, as the case may be, of the Governor of the State, any contract under which a person, not being a member of a defence service or of an all India service or of a civil service of the Union or a State, is appointed under this Constitution to hold such a post may, if the President or the Governor as the

case may be, deems it necessary in order to secure the services of a person having special qualifications, provide for the payment to him of compensation, if before the expiration of an agreed period, that post is abolished or he is, for reasons not connected with any misconduct on his part, required to vacate that post

Article 311- Dismissal, removal or reduction in rank of persons employed in civil capacities under the Union or a State

(1) No person who is a member of a civil service of the Union or an all India service or a civil service of a State or holds a civil post under the Union or a State shall be dismissed or removed by a authority subordinate to that by which he was appointed

(2) No such person as aforesaid shall be dismissed or removed or reduced in rank except after an inquiry in which he has been informed of the charges against him and given a reasonable opportunity of being heard in respect of those charges Provided that where it is proposed after such inquiry, to impose upon him any such penalty, such penalty may be imposed on the basis of the evidence adduced during such inquiry and it shall not be necessary to give such person any opportunity of making representation on the penalty proposed: Provided further that this clause shall not apply

(a) where a person is dismissed or removed or reduced in rank on the ground of conduct which has led to his conviction on a criminal charge; or

(b) where the authority empowered to dismiss or remove a person or to reduce him in rank ins satisfied that for some reason, to be recorded by that authority in writing, it is not reasonably practicable to hold such inquiry; or

(c) where the President or the Governor, as the case may be, is satisfied that in the interest of the security of the State, it is not expedient to hold such inquiry

(3) If, in respect of any such person as aforesaid, a question arises whether it is reasonably practicable to hold such inquiry as is referred to in clause (2), the decision thereon of the authority empowered to dismiss or remove such person or to reduce him in rank shall be final

Steps in Involved in Disciplinary Proceeding.

- calling for an explanation
- framing of charges if in the case explanation is not forthcoming or is unsatisfactory
- Suspension of the employees
- Hearing of the charges and giving opportunity to defend
- Findings and report
- Giving another opportunity to defend against the proposed punishment

- Punishment order or exoneration

- Appeal if any.

True 'appeal boards' are to be distinguished from the above mentioned 'trial boards', in that the former are invoked only at the behest of the employee after disciplinary action, whereas the latter constitute the instrument by which the initial action itself may be decided on and taken.[51]

As regard the power to hear appeal an employee appointed by the president has no right to appeal from an order passed by the president himself. Only after all the remedies available to the employee under the service rules have been tried and exhausted then finally an appeal to the courts of law against wrongful removal or dismissal can always be made.

Issues and Problems

1. Lack of knowledge of disciplinary procedure

2. Delays

3. Lack of fair play

4. Withholding of Appeal

5. Too many rules

6. Lack of proper understanding

7. Lack of tolerance

8. Lack of standards expected from employees.

9. Attitude of the supervisor

10. Inconsistency

11. Absence of constructive element.

According to Pigors and Myers 'constructive discipline' starts with an effort to foster mutual understanding and an organizational centered view; demonstrably consistent with sound principles of human relations (including due process and the rights of appeal); in accord with the policy statement on discipline which is clear and well known to all; implements ideas that have been worked out by conferring with representatives of those who are subject to discipline; and takes account of any extenuating features in each situation where some one feels that discipline is called for.[52]

EMPLOYEE AND EMPLOYER RELATIONS

Employee and employer relationship is vital for the organization as the quality and quantity of work depends on this relationship. Conflict resolution management helps foster cordial relations and takes away the tension from the winds of both. In government organization because of its sheer size direct employee- employer contact is difficult but both of them act through institutional framework.

Employees Association and Union

Unionism springs from the basic aspirations of those employees who become convinced that they can gain more through membership in a union than by going at it along.[53] It is an important tool for employees welfare. Government instead of taking stringent role becomes liberal in treating its employees. The sense of association gives employees feeling of security, courage and ensures better service conditions. It also helps in complaint and grievance redressal. The different and diverse needs of the civil service can be addressed only through collective representation and bargaining.

Objectives

- Secure fair wages and improve their opportunities for promotion and training.

- Safeguard security of tenure and improve their conditions of service.
- Improve working and living conditions of workers.
- Provide them educational, cultural and recreational facilities.
- Facilitate technological advancement by broadening the understanding of employees.
- Help them in improving levels of production, productivity, discipline and high standard of living.
- Promote individual and collective welfare and thus correlate the employee's interests with that of the organization.
- Avenue to gauge employee opinion on issues.
- Foster sense of belonging and team spirit.

Growth

Employees association and unions in public services is of recent origin than the professional associations like medical association, etc. However it growth is widespread and extensive. The causes are the emergence of welfare state; rapid expansion of public services; and cases of employee-employer conflict in civil services. The growth association and unions in civil services is still nothing in comparison to the private services it is because the different nature of the services.

The earliest known trade unions in India were the Bombay Millhand's Association formed in 1890, the Amalgamated

Society of railway servants of India and Burma formed in 1897, Printers' Union formed in Calcutta in 1905, the Bombay Postal Union which was formed in 1907, the *Kamgar Hitwardhak Sabha* Bombay formed in 1910. Trade Union movement began in India after the end of First World War. After a decade following the end of First World War the pressing need for the coordination of the activities of the individual unions was recognized.[54] The establishment of the International Labour Organization in 1917 was also a watershed development for protecting the interest of the working class all over the world. The ILO brought new vision and new focus on issues which were affecting employment, working conditions, social security, rights of workers and employers, occupational health and safety.[55] Thus, the All India Trade Union Congress was formed in 1920 on a National Basis, the Central Labour Board, Bombay and the Bengal Trades Union Federation was formed in 1922. The All India Railway men's Federation was formed in the same year and this was followed by the creation of both Provincial and Central federations of unions of postal and telegraph employees.[56] The Indian civil service Association 1918.[57] It was in 1926 that the Indian Trade Unions Act was passed. For the safeguard of the rights of the labour class, the Indian Trade Unions Bill, 1925 was introduced in the Central Legislative

Assembly to provide for the registration of Trade Unions and in certain respects to define the law relating to registered Trade Unions in Provinces of India. The Indian Trade Unions Bill, 1925 having been passed by the Legislature received its assent on 25th March, 1926. It came into force on 1st June, 1927 as the Indian Trade Unions Act, 1926 (16 of 1926). By section 3 of the Indian Trade Unions (Amendment) Act, 1964 (38 of 1964) the word "Indian" has been omitted and now it is known as The Trade Unions Act, 1926 (16 of 1926).[58] Income tax officers association was initially a federative body of the associations at the State level, and was named as "All India Federation of Income Tax Gazetted Services Associations." After the promulgation of the Recognition of Service Association Rules 1993, by the Government of India, the name of association was first changed to "Income Tax Gazetted Services Federation (ITGSF)" and subsequently to the present name of "Income Tax Gazetted Officers Association (ITGOA)". The revised Recognition Rules necessitated change of our structure too, from a federative body to a unitary body[59] All India Audit and Accounts Association was founded on 15th April 1923[60]

Right to Form Union and Associations

Article 19(1) of the constitution of India guarantees that (1) All citizens shall have the right (c) to form associations or unions.

97

It is a fundamental right enshrined in the constitution that is applicable to the government employees to form association for protecting their service condition.

Restriction on Right to Join Employees Unions

The Indian trade union act 1926 and the constitution of India 1950 permitted the employees to form into associations but it is linked with the recognition. The All India Services Rules, 1968 and the Civil Services (Conduct) Rules, 1964 has restricted the right to join unions. Government servant can join association which has within a period of 6 months from its formation obtained the recognition of the government under the rules prescribed in that behalf. According to the conduct rules no government servant shall join or continue to be a member of any service association of government servants, recognition in respect of which has been refused or with drawn by the government under the said rules. The provisions of Indian trade union Act 1926 did not extend to the civil servants. Former employees and retired ones are allowed in civil service association.

Right to Strike

The right to strike is resorted by the public servants in almost all the countries like America, France, England, Canada, Australia, Japan, India and so on, despite it is allowed or not. There is no law prohibiting the public servant from strike in

England. Public servant has right to strike in France. In Germany under the law public servants right to strike does not exist. One may lose employment for violation of laws. Non-industrial public servants are denied the right to strike in India. Under the provisions of the Act of 1947 strikes by the Government Servants in America had been declared illegal. Penalties or punishments are imposed for illegal strikes as per the service conditions and conduct rules followed by various countries.

Arguments for Right to Strike- Proprietary functions of government can be undertaken by the private industry in much better manner than the government. It has strongly been argued, that since there are counterparts of these employees in the private sector who are allowed to strike, the public employees should also have the right to strike.

It is difficult to comprehend that strikes by private employees are not considered *ipso facto* harmful to the employer, but strikes by public employees are.

All those who work for the government are not involved in civic amenities, health and law and order related work.

The argument of 'sovereignty' which compels the obeisance of the serf to the lord, who rules by divine right, is deeply rooted in medieval mythology. It certainly does not have place in a complex industrial civilization. Thus the government which

99

asserts that "I am the people," will invite the reply from the workers, "Who do you think we are?"[61]

The sovereignty argument was originally proposed in a political context. While strikes though often have political overtones, their basic motivation is economic. A strike thus cannot be equated with anarchy, but rather with an expression of a grievance.[62]

Arguments Against Right to Strike- There are four basic arguments voiced by those in favor of not allowing public employees to have the right to strike. They are as follows[63]

1. There is no profit motive in state government.

2. The public employees are agents of the government and they are invested with a fiduciary responsibility not to violate that trust.

3. Strikes by public employees will lead to harmful consequences, such as loss of police and/or fire protection.

4. The State is the sovereign, and the sovereign cannot be struck.

Machinery for Employee - Employer Dialogue

In almost all the countries there is no right to strike and hence there should be some machinery for conflict and grievance management. The institutional provision available for this in various countries is discussed here.

In UK - Whitley Council

When in 1917 the Ministry of Labour published the "Report of the Departmental Reconstruction Committee on the Relations of Employers and Employed," it was thought in some quarters that the application of the principles of that report might inaugurate a new epoch in industry. Many people hailed the coming of what was soon called Whitleyism as a savior from Industrial Anarchy on the one hand and from Socialism on the other. In 1922, no one thinks that a new epoch in industry has come, and no one really thinks that Whitleyism will save industry from any of the ills that beset it. Four years have been more than enough to destroy the credit of Industrial Whitleyism. Yet Whitleyism is still alive and shows signs of vigor, not in that industrial system for which it was devised, but in an environment that many people declared to be wholly unsuitable to its operation. In the Civil Service, the Whitley System has taken root and has developed an extraordinarily complex organization in the short space of a couple of years. It is no exaggeration to say that no more elaborate system has been devised in the history of Conciliation.

This Committee, under the Chairmanship of the John Henry Whitley, had been appointed during the War to find some way of dealing with the very serious unrest in industry; this unrest was, perhaps, no greater than at other times, but it forced itself on the attention of the Government because, owing to the peculiar conditions of the time the work-people happened to be almost as strong as their employers, and because the conduct of the war depended so much on the smooth working of industry.

In its report, the Committee laid stress on the importance of:

(a) Adequate organization on the part of employers and employed.

(b) Greater opportunity of participating in the discussion about and adjustment of those parts of industry by which they are most affected, of the work-people in each occupation.

(c) Subordination of any decisions to those of the Trade Unions and Employers' Associations.

The constitution recommended by the Committee laid down the functions of the National Whitley Council in terms closely following those of the original Whitley report, and specified them as being the securing of:

1. Provision of the best means for utilizing the ideas and experience of the staff

2. Means for securing to the staff a greater share in and responsibility for the determination and observance of the conditions under which their duties are carried out.

3. Determination of the general principles governing conditions of service, e.g., recruitment, hours, promotion, discipline, tenure, remuneration and superannuation

4. The encouragement of the further education of civil servants and their training in higher administration and organization

5. Improvement of office machinery and organization and the provision of opportunities for the full consideration of suggestions by the staff on this subject

6. Proposed legislation so far as it has a bearing upon the position of Civil Servants in relation to their employment

In place of the original proposal that the Council should be merely consultative and advisory, it was provided that:

"The decisions of the Council shall be arrived at by agreement between the two sides, shall be signed by the Chairman and Vice-Chairman, shall be reported to the Cabinet, and thereupon shall become operative."

This is a vital clause. It ensures that the Council shall not be a place for the mere pronouncing of pious opinions; it gives weight to its deliberations and prevents them from being ignored.[64]

Organization of Whitley Council

Three tier structures consists of council at

National Council

- The national council consists of fifty four members half of them appointed by government to form official side and half by groups of staff associations to constitute staff side.

- Members of both sides must be persons of standing who may or may not be Civil Servants
- Chairman - officer while vice-chairman is an employee and two secretaries from each side.

Departmental Council

- The same formula applies to the official sides of departmental councils as to the national council. The HOD or minister appoints official side of the council. Members of the staff side are appointed by the association or group of associations having members employed in the department.
- Chairman is HOD and secretary is usually a senior member of establishment division.

Local Councils

- Local head of units chairman
- Other members are appointed by recognized associations.

Although the national council approves the membership of departmental council there is no hierarchical relation between the national council and department council. Functionally there is some relation, as the national council also looks after the interdepartmental matter.

Proceedings

- Council meets once in three months.

- Council follows committee pattern, in matters of importance a meeting of the full council takes place. Decisions are derived by consensus.
- Agreed minutes of national council duly signed by chairman and vice-chairman are reported to cabinet and thereupon becomes operational.
- There is no provision for voting on matters that arise.

Limitations

- Does not relieve government as it is responsible to parliament.
- Whitley mechanism does not rule out direct negotiation between the government and the staff association as happens in case of class or grade remuneration.
- The councils do not consider individual cases they discuss only the principles underlying such cases.

Arbitration

On February 21st, 1922, the Chairman, Vice-Chairman and Secretaries of the National Council were summoned to meet the Chancellor of the Exchequer. They were then informed that the Cabinet had decided to abolish the Arbitration Board and also to alter the composition of the Official Side by placing M.P.'s upon it. The announcement took the Staff representatives completely by surprise. It was repeated publicly the next day in the House of Commons when, in reply to a question, Sir Robert Horne made the following statement: "His Majesty's Government have been considering this matter. The conditions which led to the establishment of the Civil Service Arbitration Board some five years ago have been entirely changed by the formation of Whitley Councils for the discussion of questions affecting the remuneration and conditions of service of civil servants; and the Government have come to the conclusion that the continuance of the present arrangements for compulsory arbitration are inconsistent with, and to some extent militate against, the development of these Councils on the best lines. They have accordingly decided that the time has now come for bringing the present arbitration arrangements to an end. They have decided, also, that under these altered conditions it would be desirable to strengthen the National Whitley Council for the Civil Service by the appointment of some Members of this House who would form part of the Official Side." With these the arbitration boards have disappeared with the institution of Whitley council.[65]

In USA- Alternative Dispute Resolution (ADR)[66]

The first uses of alternative dispute resolution (ADR) processes began experimentally in the 1970's as a potential remedy for disabling court backlogs, and as resolution techniques for environmental and natural resource disputes. A number of initiatives by Congress and the Government have encouraged the use of alternative methods of workplace dispute resolution throughout the Executive Branch. In the 1990's, Congress passed three statutes (the Administrative Dispute Resolution Acts of 1990 and 1996, and the Alternative Dispute Resolution Act of 1998) which, collectively, required each agency to adopt a policy encouraging use of ADR in a broad range of decision making, and required the federal trial courts to make ADR programs available to litigants. Alternative dispute resolution (ADR) consists of a variety of approaches to early intervention and dispute resolution. Many of these approaches include the use of a neutral individual such as a mediator who can assist disputing parties in resolving their disagreements. ADR increases the parties' opportunities to resolve disputes prior to or during the use of formal administrative procedures and litigation (which can be very costly and time-consuming). It typically is not intended to replace the more traditional approaches and it can provide long term solutions to employee-employer conflicts through stakeholders' participation and buy-in. In contrast, traditional dispute resolution procedures often impose a "solution" handed down by a third party (e.g., a judge), where neither party walks away satisfied, and the disputing parties' conflict continues or increases. ADR has most commonly taken the form of mediation. However, there are many other options available including conciliation, cooperative problem-solving, dispute panels, facilitation, fact finding, interest-based problem solving and bargaining, settlement conferences, ombudsing, peer review, and alternative discipline. Parties can use any of these ADR techniques, combinations of them, or others. In short, parties can design and implement virtually any form of ADR which suits their needs.

Benefits of ADR- There are many benefits to alternative dispute resolution (ADR), including

- Complaints are processed more quickly and resolved earlier

- The process leads to more creative solutions

- Savings in time of attorneys, staff, and parties who are federal employees

- Quicker resolution than a hearing would offer and less time that the parties have spent under the cloud of pending litigation

- Creative resolutions acceptable to the parties, but which a third-party reviewer could not impose

- A durable and voluntary agreement.

Moreover, even in the cases which do not results in resolution, other distinct advantages to the ADR process include

- Laying the groundwork for a subsequent settlement

- Increasing clarification of the issues for third-party review.

In India- Joint Consultative Machinery (JCM)

The scheme of Joint Consultative Machinery is a platform for constructive dialogue between the representatives of the staff side and the official side for peaceful resolution of all disputes between the Government as employer and the employees. The scheme was introduced in 1966 with the objectives of promoting harmonious relations and securing the greatest measure of cooperation between the Central Government as the employer and the employees in matters of common concern and with the object of further increasing the efficiency of the public service combined with the well being of those employed. The scheme is a non statutory one mutually agreed upon between the staff side and the official side. The scheme covers all regular civil employees of the Central Government, except:

(a)The Class –I (Group-A) services;

(b)The Class-II (Group-B) services, other than the Central Secretariat Services and the other comparable services in the headquarters organization of the Government;

(c) Persons in industrial establishments employed mainly in managerial or administrative capacity, and those who being employed in supervisory capacity drawing salary going beyond grade pay of Rs.4200/- per month;

(d)Employees of the Union Territories; and

(e)Police personnel

The scheme provides for setting up of Joint Councils at the National, Departmental and Regional / Office levels. The National Council, chaired by the Cabinet Secretary, is the apex body. The representatives of the staff side for various Joint Councils are chosen / selected from members of the recognized service associations/ unions. As per the JCM Scheme, ordinary meeting of the National Council/ Departmental Council may be held as often as necessary as but not less than once in four months. The Department of Personnel & Training being the nodal department for matters relating to Joint Consultative Machinery and Compulsory Arbitration has notified Central Civil Services (Recognition of Associations) Rules, 1993 for the purpose of granting recognition to various service associations. Recognition is actually granted by the concerned Ministry/ Department in accordance with the CCS (RSA) Rules, 1993. In case of any doubt or confusion, the matter is referred to the JCA Section of the Department of Personnel and Training for clarification/ advice. The recognized associations/ unions enjoy certain facilities like:

(a) Negotiations with the employer;

(b)Correspondence and meetings with the head of the administrative departments;

(c)Provision of accommodation for the associations subject to availability;

(d)Facility of special casual leave up to 20 days in a year to the office bearers of the associations;

(e)Payment of T.A/ D.A for attending officially sponsored meetings; and

(f) Facility of seeking transfer of Chief Executive of the Union / association to the Headquarters of the appropriate head of administration.

If there is no agreement between the staff and the official side on an arbitrable issue, then the matter is to be referred to the Board of Arbitration if so desired by the staff side. The arbitration is limited to the following issues:

(a) Pay and allowances;

(b)Weekly hours of work; and

(c) Leave

The award given by the Board of Arbitration is binding on the Government as well as the staff side subject to the overriding authority of the Parliament. The award can be modified/ rejected only with the approval of the Parliament through a formal resolution on grounds affecting national economy or social justice.[67]

BUREAUCRACY

Origin of the Term

The term bureaucracy is derived from bureau which literally means "desk with drawers, writing desk," from French *bureau* "office; desk, writing table," originally "cloth covering for a desk," from *burel* "coarse woolen cloth" used as a cover for writing desks, old French diminutive of *bure* "dark brown cloth," which is perhaps either from Latin *burrus* "red," or from Late Latin *burra* "wool, shaggy garment." Offices being full of such desks, the meaning expanded in 1720 to "division of a government." [68] It was in 1818 French economist Jean Claude Marie Vincent de Gournay coined *bureaucratie* on model of *democratie, aristocratie*, by adding Greek suffix *kratia* denoting "power of." Some thinkers believe that the term though popularized in France originated in Germany. During reporting about the French revolution, German newspaper used the term. In France, the term was first popularized by the novelist and playwright, Honoré de Balzac considered as one of the founding fathers of realism in European Literature. Later the term bureaucracy came to be known as *bureaukratie* in France, became the *bureaukaratie* in Germany, *burocrazia* in Italy and bureaucracy in the English speaking world.

Meaning of Bureaucracy

The term bureaucracy soon acquired so many significations that it can now be used without much sense of strain for about forty marginally differentiated senses, falling under ten headings. Since this situation is not untypical for many words—some have far more meanings—that are frequently used by contemporary social scientists, 'bureaucracy' is rather a shifty, but not untypical, word.[69]

The term 'bureaucracy' was originally used as derogatory. It was Max Weber who gave bureaucracy positive overtones. The perverse sense from it was removed by efforts of scholars who started using it with more powerful appeal relating it to the propriety of official action. At first bureaucracy was used only to designate existing phenomena and now it stands with the identity manifested by its attributes. Bureaucracy is now a concrete entity. The meaning for bureaucracy given by various authors is summarized below.

Bureaucratic Polity- According to J. S. Mill, The work of government has been in the hands of governors by profession: which is the essence and meaning of bureaucracy.[70] Harold Laski writing on bureaucracy in the Encyclopedia of the Social Sciences points that the bureaucracy is a system of government, the control of which is so completely in the hands of officials that their power jeopardizes the liberties of ordinary citizens.[71] Herman Finer, defines bureaucracy as government by officials.[72] To Lasswell and Kaplan it is the form of rule in which the elite is composed of officials.[73] Bureaucracy is no longer used in this sense.

Bureaucrats in Power- Bureaucrats in power is the evolution from the bureaucratic polity, bureaucracy is viewed as a ruling class of officials.[74] The conceptual construct of 'bureaucratic absolutism' postulates schism in rulers and ruled and ruling class is further distinguished as feudal and bureaucratic which necessarily is bureaucracy in modern state.[75] Robert Michels views bureaucrats as power elite and includes salaried professionals in non-governmental voluntary organizations as well as in government. Michels prefers the word 'organization' to 'bureaucracy.'[76] Bureaucracy means the exercise of power by professionalized administrators. Ramsay Muir wrote that the most steady, persistent, and powerful influences in the government of England are those of the great permanent officials.[77] Bureaucracy is the exercise of power by professional administrators.[78] The increasingly influential power of officials in fact is of sociological significance that the bureaucracy should be reserved for it alone. Bureaucracy means government by officials, in the context of power play by the office-holders.[79]

Office Holders- Bureaucracy is a class of office-holders and they may or may not have power. This is reflected in writings of J. S. Mill,[80] Eduard Fischel,[81] and Michels.[82] The next evolutionary step occurs when bureaucracy is criticized for its inefficiency. Friedrich von Schulte wrote about the differences between the bureaucracy and the citizenry emphasizing that everybody blames the Bureaucracy and asks from it everything he needs.[83] Walter Bagehot wrote that a skilled bureaucracy—a bureaucracy trained from early life to its special avocation... in a context that deplored its lack of efficiency rather than its abuse of power.[84] It was Max Weber who remains the proponent of bureaucracy as a class of officeholders though it is not reflected in weberian ideal construct of bureaucracy. Weber did not defined unequivocally the term bureaucracy as a body of appointed officials, but it becomes evident when he wrote that no exercise of authority can be purely bureaucratic, i.e. purely through contractually engaged and appointed officials.[85] Bureaucrats as office-holders was used by Taylor Cole[86] and Joseph LaPalombara.[87] Joseph LaPalombara used the term to encompass all public servants.

Bureaucracy as an Apparatus- Bureaucracy is viewed not only class of officials but also organization in which they serve i.e. state. Bureaucracy is a civil institution analogous to the standing army.[88] Fritz Morstein Marx defines bureaucracy to mean the type of organization used by modern government for the conduct of various specialized functions, embodied in the administrative system.[89] It is the administrative side of the governmental political system. Those who think of bureaucracy as an apparatus think of it as possessing principles of organization.

Bureaucracy as an Ideal Construct- Max Weber's bureaucracy is a normative paradigmatic definition of attributes. It should not be confused with any real world functioning organization. The weberian conceptualization uses the term bureaucracy to mean office holders. The characteristics of ideal type of bureaucracy includes hierarchy, impersonality, division of labour, professional qualifications as basis for selection and recruitment, career system, salaries written documents based administration, etc.

Bureaucracy as Pathogenesis- In the writings on bureaucracy the term is expressed pejoratively. The dysfunctional aspects of bureaucracy like red tape, delays, rigid rule orientation, circumlocution, etc., are often emphasized in the writings on the bureaucratic behavior. Reinhard Bendix in his essay published in International Encyclopedia of the Social Sciences on Bureaucracy identifies the following organizational characteristics: failure to allocate responsibility clearly, rigid rules and routines, blundering officials, slow operation and buck-passing, conflicting directives, empire building, concentration of control in the hands of a few.[90] Webster's new international dictionary defines bureaucracy as a system of administration marked by constant striving for increased functions and power, by lack of initiative and flexibility, by indifference to human needs or public opinion, and by a tendency to defer decisions to superiors or to impede action with red tape. The negative characterization of bureaucracy is termed as 'Patho-bureaucracy.'

Bureaucracy as an Organization or Staff- Social studies on government do not take into account entire state but the focus is on behavior. The term organization than is used synonymously with bureaucracy. One of the most salient structural characteristics of such a society is the prominence in it of relatively large-scale organizations with specialized functions, what rather loosely tend to be called bureaucracies.[91] Charles Hyneman also gives his opinion that bureaucracy as an abstraction is big organization, and any big organization is specifically a bureaucracy.[92] Any big, large, complex organization possesses staff but bureaucracy is rarely used in this sense by industrial organizations.

Bureaucracy as Society- In addition to the meaning of bureaucracy discussed above it also means a social system or society. Many of the political concepts like 'democracy' that we use are used loosely to denote interpersonal or social relations. It holds true to the idea of bureaucratic polity, domination of bureaucracy has marked influence on society and pervade all interrelationships. It is depicted in the writings of Karl Wittfogel[93] and James Burnham.[94] Presthus analysis echoes bureaucratic society when he writes that the organizational society has emerged, characterized by large-scale bureaucratic institutions in virtually every social area.[95] Albrow argues that since Presthus regards 'big organizations' and 'bureaucratic structures' as synonyms, 'we can conclude that it is not incongruous to think of bureaucracy as a type of society.'[96] Other authors who offer distinctive perspective though they don't exactly use bureaucracy to mean a bureaucratic society are, Bruno Rizzi,[97] Max Schachtman,[98] Milovan Djilas,[99] and Karl Mannheim.[100]

Bureaucracy as 'Bureaucratism' or 'Bureaupathology'- A derogatory conception of bureaucracy as apparent bad administration is depicted in the novel *Les Employés* of Honoré de Balzac published in 1836 where it bitterly states that the bureaucracy, the giant power wielded by pigmies...a natural kindness for mediocrity, a predilection for categorical statements and reports...as fussy and meddlesome, in short, as a small shopkeeper's wife.[101] It was Robert von Mohl who used in 1862 the word 'bureaucratism' to denote the false conception of the tasks of the state, implemented by a numerous...body of professional officials.[102] Polish writer, Josef Olszewski used the term 'bureaucratism' to refer to the offensive attitudes and behaviour of officials.[103] According to Albrow, French sociologist, Frederic Le Play, writing in 1860, used bureaucracy, to mean the dissemination of authority among minor officials, absorbed in details, intent upon complicating business, and suppressing initiative in others.[104] Bureaucracy to Marshall Dimock, is the composite institutional manifestations which tend towards inflexibility and depersonalization.[105] Strauss referred to bureaucracy as the many imperfections in the structure and functioning of big organizations.[106] To Michel Crozier, it is mal-adaptations, the inadequacies, or... the dysfunctions which necessarily develop within human organizations. He further writes that the word evokes notions of ponderousness, the routine, the complication of procedures, and the maladapted responses of bureaucratic organizations.[107] It was Victor Thompson who first used the word 'bureau-pathology'. It denotes the dysfunctional defects of the conscientious efforts made by officials to fulfil the legal rational role. Whereas von Mohl's 'bureaucratism' emphasis the subjectively irrational behaviour of officials, their corruption, pettiness, rigidity, etc. which leads to socially objectionable results.[108]

Bureaucracy and Rationality- Weber's legal rational domination highlights the functional, achievement centric universal behavioural norms. The concept of rationality involves cost-effectiveness or productivity in administration. The word rational denotes legal rational in weberian parlance and rational in the administrative usage. The rational connotations are reflected in definition given by Peter Blau of bureaucracy, as organization that maximizes efficiency in administration.[109] Bureaucracy means that mode of organizing which is peculiarly well adapted to maintaining stability and efficiency in organizations that are large and complex.[110] It refers to the rational and clearly defined arrangement of activities which are directed towards fulfilling the purposes of the organization.[111]

Thus Bureaucracy is characterized as possessing both negative and positive features. It is reflected in the dictionary meaning.

"Systematic administration characterized by specializations of functions, objective qualification for office, action according to fixed rules and a hierarchy of authority."

-Webster's dictionary

"The term usually applied to a system of government, the control of which is so completely in the hands of officials that their power jeopardizes the liberties of ordinary citizens."

-Encyclopedia of Social Sciences by Laski

Types of Bureaucracy

Bureaucracy can be categorized into seven types.

Guardian Bureaucracy- Plato's guardians or philosopher kings were responsible for welfare and justice in the city state. They were managers of society. Guardians were those individuals who specialize in statecraft. At the end of Book V Plato describes the way of life of the guardians of the republic.

"Then let us consider what will be their way of life, if they are to realize our idea of them. In the first place, none of them should have any property of his own beyond what is absolutely necessary; neither should they have a private house or store closed against anyone who has a mind to enter; their provisions should be only such as are required by trained warriors, who are men of temperance and courage; they should agree to receive from the citizens a fixed rate of pay, enough to meet the expenses of the year and no more; and they will go and live together like soldiers in a camp. Gold and silver we will tell them that they have from God; the diviner metal is within them, and they have therefore no need of the dross which is current among men, and ought not to pollute the divine by any such earthly admixture; for that commoner metal has been the source of many unholy deeds, but their own is undefiled. And they alone of all the citizens may not touch or handle silver or

gold, or be under the same roof with them, or wear them, or drink from them. And this will be their salvation, and they will be the saviours of the State. But should they ever acquire homes or lands or moneys of their own, they will become housekeepers and husbandmen instead of guardians, enemies and tyrants instead of allies of the other citizens; hating and being hated, plotting and being plotted against, they will pass their whole life in much greater terror of internal than of external enemies, and the hour of ruin, both to themselves and to the rest of the State, will be at hand. For all which reasons may we not say that thus shall our State be ordered, and that these shall be the regulations appointed by us for guardians concerning their houses and all other matters?"

The guardian bureaucracy is likely to become unresponsive to public opinion, detached from the public affairs and day to day problems.

Caste Bureaucracy- In this type of bureaucracy persons belonging to particular castes are included. Caste bureaucracy arises from the class connections of those in the controlling positions. This bureaucracy also manifests itself by linking the qualifications for the higher posts with arrangements that amount to class preference. It is similar to the Willoughby's aristocratic bureaucracy[112] or personnel system prevalent in

England where individuals from aristocratic classes were preferred in bureaucracy. The caste bureaucracy can be found a century after Diocletian who himself came from the family of low status and rose to become Roman emperor credited for restoring efficient government. After him the administration degenerated into one with caste spirit. In ancient India also only individuals belonging to *Brahmins* and *Kshatriyas* could become officials. During Meiji constitution in Japan and 1950's France experienced caste bureaucracy.

Patronage Bureaucracy- Patronage bureaucracy is a system of giving rewards to friends and allies in exchange for their support. This type of bureaucracy is also called spoils system prevalent in USA during 1800's. The employees in the George Washington's administration were from Federalist Party towards which Washington has inclination. When Thomas Jefferson a democratic-republican came to power many of the federalists were dismissed and members of Democratic-Republican Party were given jobs. The credit to entrench the patronage or spoils system goes to President Andrew Jackson. He followed the policy of 'to the victor go the spoils' and brought 'Jacksonian Democrats' into office. He was of the opinion that the spoils system brings rotation in administration which is good for government.

Merit Bureaucracy- The system of employing and promoting civil servants solely on the basis of ability rather than patronage[113] is called as merit bureaucracy. It is a system or policy whereby people are promoted or rewarded on the basis of ability and achievement rather than because of seniority, quotas, patronage, or the like.[114] Qin dynasty, the first ruling dynasty of imperial China 221-206 BC is credited to have a centralized bureaucratic system of talented individuals. The later Han government borrowed many features of Qin dynasty. In modern times the credit to introduce merit bureaucracy goes to Prussia. The early modern Prussian bureaucracy is widely seen as the canonical example of the merit-system in practice. Prussia first introduced the use of merit-examinations for the appointment of higher civil servants to the General Directory (central bureaucracy) in 1743.[115] Exams for recruitment to judicial office had been in use for some years prior. By the first decade of the 19th Century, following the battle of Jena, requirements were introduced that all new entrant to the higher civil service have a university education, and the civil service exam was expanded to cover a wider variety of posts[116] and, by 1846, it became impossible to move from the lower to the higher civil service without passing an examination.[117] In modern times, merit bureaucracy puts strong emphasis on political control over the administration. The rationality in administrative behavior is feature of merit bureaucracy.

Representative Bureaucracy- Representative bureaucracy is an effort to instill democratic values to the public administration. The idea was first expressed by Donald Kingsley in 1944. The theory of representative bureaucracy proposes that a demographically diverse public sector workforce will lead to policy outcomes that reflect the interests of all groups represented, including historically disadvantaged communities.[118] Paul Van Riper later added the concepts of 'ethos and attitudes' as vital for representativeness to the Kingley's proposition. Van Riper explains, "A representative bureaucracy is one in which there is a minimal distinction between the bureaucrats as a group and their administrative behavior and practices on the one hand and the community or society memberships and its administrative behaviors, practices, and expectations of government on the other." Representative bureaucracy according to Paul P. Van Riper must consist of reasonable cross section of body politic in terms of occupations, class, geography and the likes. It must be in general tune with the ethos and attitudes of the society of which it is a part. In social, economic, class, geographic, educational, ethnic, religious and social characteristics, American bureaucracy is essentially a mirror of the nation. It is more responsive to public needs. The American system has successes in building a bureaucracy which is representative.[119] This new addition by Van Riper shifted the focus from "that which bureaucracy does" to "that which bureaucracy is"[120]

Balanced Bureaucracy- Effective inclusion of bureaucracy in the democratic country is possible only when it is the state of perfect 'balance.' A bureaucracy is in imbalance when it fails to operate on the basis of democratic consent. Bureaucratic imbalance may be either despotic subservient. Despotic implies that the bureaucracy is too much the master while subservient implies that it is too much the servant. Balance consists of following elements widespread knowledge about the bureaucracy; a feeling that the public's self interest is being served by the bureaucracy; a feeling that the bureaucracy provides equal treatment; and the bureaucracy must have an adequate prestige value.[121] David Nachmias and David H. Rosenbloom have advocated balance in the bureaucracy.

Participatory Bureaucracy- Participation is suited for managing the tensions between bureaucracy and democracy in context of interdependent tasks. Public engagement that offers task specific diverse expertise is participatory bureaucracy.[122] Invited guests involvement is sought for policy making in the participatory bureaucracy. Broader public engagement takes place to let public observe and participate in policy discourses.

Participatory bureaucracy is aimed at policy design and implementation. In participatory bureaucracy there is information flow in several directions that helps avoid policy failures. Participatory bureaucracy consists of four elements, representation; organizational democracy; bureaucrats to engage in deliberation and discussion; and citizen participation in bureaucratic policy making.[123] Participatory bureaucracy is different from representative bureaucracy because in participatory bureaucracy representation occurs through participation by involving outsiders in bureaucratic policy making whereas in representative bureaucracy representation is achieved by bureaucrats themselves. Participatory bureaucracy has the potential to deal with the pressure of bureaucratic administration and democratic accountability. Participation in bureaucracy is possible, when public administration is supportive and competent, and bureaucracy can be participatory when it supports democratic accountability. Participatory bureaucracy provides a form of administration beneficial simultaneously to policy implementers and political executive. Participatory bureaucracy fosters public involvement that is conducive for bureaucracy and democracy to be better placed.

Views on bureaucracy

Saint Simon's View- Henri de Saint-Simon was a French theorist often referred as utopian socialist. He was critical of public officials and referred them as the idling class that included able people who preferred to be parasitic and benefit from the work of others while seeking to avoid doing work. He regarded the principal economic roles of government as insuring that productive activity in the economy is unhindered and reducing idleness in society. He strongly criticized any expansion of government intervention into the economy beyond these two principal economic roles, saying that when the government goes beyond these roles, it becomes a "tyrannical enemy of industry" and that the industrial economy will decline as a consequence of such excessive government intervention.[124] Saint-Simon stressed the need for recognition of the merit of the individual and the need for hierarchy of merit in society and in the economy, such as society having hierarchical merit-based organizations of managers and scientists to be the decision-makers in government.[125]

Karl Marx's View- In the materialist conception of history Karl Marx attributes the origin of bureaucracy to the following Religion- Group of clergy interpreting rituals and officials maintaining order;

128

State- Law making and its implementation, levy and collection of various taxes;

Commerce- Accounting, processing, legal compliance; and

Technology- Mass production, management, technical expertise

Bureaucracy is not involved in wealth creation but it controls and coordinates the means of production, distribution, and consumption of wealth. Karl Marx in his *Critique of Hegel's philosophy of right* writes,

> *The bureaucracy is the state formalism of civil society. It is the state's consciousness, the state's will, the state's power, as a Corporation. Being the state's consciousness, will, and power as a Corporation, the bureaucracy is thus a particular, closed society within the state. The bureaucracy wills the Corporation as an imaginary power...The bureaucracy as the completed Corporation therefore wins the day over the Corporation which is like incomplete bureaucracy...The Corporation is civil society's attempt to become state; but the bureaucracy is the state which has really made itself into civil society. The state formalism, which the bureaucracy is, is the state as formalism...this state formalism constitutes itself as a real power and becomes itself its own material content, it is evident that the bureaucracy is a tissue of practical illusion, or the illusion*

of the state. The bureaucratic mind is through and through a Jesuitical, theological mind. The bureaucrats are the Jesuits and theologians of the state...since the bureaucracy according to its essence is the state as formalism, so too it is according to its end...the bureaucracy asserts itself to be the final end of the state. Because the bureaucracy makes its formal aims its content, it comes into conflict everywhere with the real aims...the aims of the state are transformed into aims of bureaus, or the aims of bureaus into the aims of the state. The bureaucracy is a circle from which no one can escape. Its hierarchy is a hierarchy of knowledge. The highest point entrusts the understanding of particulars to the lower echelons, whereas these, on the other hand, credit the highest with an understanding in regard to the universal; and thus they deceive one another.

The bureaucracy is the imaginary state alongside the real state; it is the spiritualism of the state. As a result everything has a double meaning, one real and one bureaucratic, just as knowledge is double, one real and one bureaucratic (and the same with the will)...The bureaucracy has the being of the state, the spiritual being of society, in its possession; it is its private property. The general spirit of the bureaucracy is the secret, the mystery, preserved inwardly by means of the hierarchy and externally as a closed corporation...authority is the principle of its knowledge and being, and the deification of authority is its mentality. But at the very heart of the bureaucracy this spiritualism turns into a crass materialism, the materialism of passive obedience, of trust in authority, the mechanism of an ossified and formalistic behaviour, of fixed principles, conceptions, and traditions. As far as the individual bureaucrat is concerned, the end of the state becomes his private end: a pursuit of higher posts, the building of a career...the bureaucrat has the world as a mere object of his action... The examination is nothing other than a masonic rite, the legal recognition of the privileged knowledge of state citizenship. The link of state office and individual, this objective bond between the knowledge of civil society and the knowledge of the state, in other words the examination, is nothing but the bureaucratic baptism of knowledge, the official recognition of the transubstantiation of profane into holy knowledge (it goes without saying that in the case of every examination the examiner knows all). No one ever heard of the Greek or Roman statesmen taking an examination. But then what is a Roman statesmen even as against a Prussian official![126]

Marx viewed that the State the interests of the ruling or the dominant class that is a part of the civil society and notes that the bureaucracy is aligned with the dominant class and it thrusts on society the interests of dominant class as though the general interest. According to Marx bureaucracy is the political manifestation of the division of labor and it is vital to understand its structure and function. Marx calls France as the abode to bureaucracy.

Max Weber's View- Weber was the first social scientist who made a systematic study of bureaucracy. To Weber bureaucracy is 'an administrative body of appointed officials.' Weber's theory of bureaucracy stems from his theory of domination. Domination that is the authoritarian power to command and its basic premise is discussed in his theory. He laid down three types of domination,

- Traditional domination - It is based on the belief that what is customary is right.
- Charismatic domination- It is by virtue of possession of charisma or an exceptional quality.
- Legal Rational Domination- It is based on the belief of people in the rightness of law.

Weber's formulation of bureaucracy is an ideal type construct. The characteristics of ideal-rational bureaucracy includes impersonality, hierarchy, division of labour, selection and recruitment, career system, money salaries, written documents, rules, officials are appointed on basis of a contract, the officials post as sole or major occupation. According to Martin Albrow these ten features[127] constituted Max Weber's ideal, pure or most rational type of bureaucracy.

Growth of Bureaucracy

The factors that have contributed to the rise of bureaucracy are as under

According to Harold Laski

- The objection to aristocracy and liking for popular governments transformed power to public officials.

- Monarchy's desire to have a body of personal servants as a safeguard against aristocracy's thirst for power

- The advent of democracy in 19th century western world overthrew the class of permanent hereditary officials and this condition brought in its wake the need to have a body of experts in charge of government departments

- The enormous size of modern state and the multitude of services it catered made it imperative to have expert administration.

According to Martin Krygier [128]

- Establishment of strong centralized states in Europe
- Industrial Revolution
- Expansion in State activities
- French Revolution

- Growth of the concept that views public officials as 'public servants' of the nation and not of the rulers
- Sovereignty of Nation and not of ruler
- Money salaries to public servants made them answerable to the state and not the ruler

According to Max Weber [129]

- The creation of money economy
- The emergence of capitalist economy
- Trend towards rationality in western world
- Democracy
- Population growth in Europe
- Complex administrative tasks
- Modern forms of communication

The increase in population leads to the increasing need for civic amenities and provision for welfare measures for the people from the government that has resulted in the expansion of bureaucracy. Development of industry, trade, and commerce has resulted in creation of various government agencies for its tax collection, regulation, and monitoring apart from government in business running big public undertakings all this have resulted in the growth of bureaucracy. The emergence of welfare state and expansion of its functions has led to the expansion of bureaucracy, particularly in developing world it has resulted in multifarious proportions.

Features of Bureaucracy

1) Division labour- The complete job of organization is broken down into various specialized functions.

2) Hierarchy- The members of bureaucracy are ranked according to relative status or authority.

3) System of rules- The functioning of bureaucracy is governed by explicit rules to avoid ambiguity and foster efficiency.

4) Role specificity and job description- Conditions peculiar to particular role that is to be performed are made available. Functions and responsibilities of a position are explicitly spelt out.

5) Rationality- Bureaucracy is a rational organization. Decisions are based on supportive data that could be validated and in doing so available alternatives are considered.

6) Impersonality- Bureaucracy is a mechanical in nature and no facets of personality like emotions, connections, relations, etc be allowed to influence the working.

7) Rule orientation- Clearly laid down rules and regulations are to be followed in discharging duties to achieve depersonalization.

8) Neutrality- This implies unbiased thinking neutral to political ideology. Bureaucracy can serve any one who comes to power without making any commitments to the values of government.

Demerits of Bureaucracy

1) Bureaucracy makes public administration insensitive and irresponsible to public opinion

2) Bureaucracy results into an elite class of public servants entrenched in self aggrandizement, indifferent to the societal interest.

3) All the defects of militarism are present in this system which makes public officials unresponsive and hostile to common man

4) Bureaucracy is negation of individual freedom and it was always been a potent tool in the hands of oppressive, despotic, unjust rule throughout the history.

5) Bureaucrats are deliberately vague and evasive, embedded in routine, repetitive work instead of innovative and dynamic.

6) Bureaucracy has structural and behavioural dysfunctional aspects like red tapism, formalism, unresponsiveness, apathetic, power monger, etc

Need for Control

The effective measures to control the undesirable consequences of bureaucracy are as fallows.

1) Effective control by the political executive

2) Internal executive control

3) Develop transparency and flexibility in organizations

4) Bureaucracy should be made accountable and undue protection and safeguards for bureaucratic actions be removed.

5) Participation and representativeness will make it responsive to public needs.

6) Control over delegated authority, discretionary powers through periodic review

CIVIL SERVICE IN INDIA

Meaning and Genesis

Civil service is the name of an important government institution comprising the staff of central administration of the state. It is more for it stands for a spirit essential to the success of modern Democracy an ideal of vocation in public officials who devote their lives to the service of the community.[130] The function of the civil service in modern state is not merely the improvement of government; without it, indeed, government itself would be impossible. The civil service is a professional body of officials, permanent, paid, and skilled.[131] Civil service, the body of government officials who are employed in civil occupations that are neither political nor judicial. In most countries the term refers to employees selected and promoted on the basis of a merit and seniority system, which may include examinations.[132] The service responsible for the public administration of the government of a country. It excludes the legislative, judicial, and military branches. Members of the civil service have no official political allegiance and are not generally affected by changes of governments.[133]

In modern times the Northcote and Trevelyan's report published in February 1854, recommended civil service system based on examination and promotion on merit through open competition. It was, as historian Lord Hennessy has stated that the greatest single governing gift of the nineteenth to the twentieth century: a politically disinterested and permanent civil service with core values of integrity, propriety, objectivity and appointment on merit, able to transfer its loyalty and expertise from one elected government to the next.[134] Further the Ridley Commission 1890, the MacDonnell Commission 1914, the Gladstone Commission 1918, the Haldane report 1918, and the Tomlin Commission 1931 also made very important recommendations regarding civil services.

Role - Models for Civil Services in India

Instrumentality Role- In parliamentary democracy executive is accountable to the legislature and it is this philosophy that subsumes the subordination of the administrative system to the political control. The professional civil service is structurally and functionally evolved and strengthened so as to respond thoroughly and readily to political control and policy considerations.

Neutrality Role- Traditionally civil service is politically neutral serving governments of varied political complexions. Civil services duty is to the government of the day regardless of personal political values. The civil service must be guided by impartial advice, moral considerations and professional judgment in cases of policy preferences. Though criticized as ambiguous, civil services have to be neutral in their position and functions.

Commitment Role- Today policy making is more complex than it was during the times of emergence of the concept of neutrality. Then politics was also consensual unlike what we witness today. The complex nature of policy making requires expertise and specializations thereby involving civil service in policy making process which essentially is political value determination. Ridley has suggested that in the age of energetic pursuit of policies what is required is commitment- 'conviction civil servants.' In this scenario civil servants are expected to demonstrate commitment responsibly and responsively towards the policy objectives and values cherished in the constitution.

Impersonality Role- Impersonal role is not to have personal subject. The operations, nature and the state of civil servants are without reference to him or by which they can be affected. According to Whitehall civil servants are to be 'faceless', impersonal. Civil service should administer irrespective to status, condition, relations, and influence of the affected individuals.

Anonymity Role- The inextricable uniqueness of permanence, neutrality and anonymity forms the edifice of the doctrine of ministerial responsibility that makes minister personally liable for all the good and bad of the ministry and therefore also for all the actions and inactions of civil servants. According to Kingdom, the very heart of democratic theory... civil servants are not themselves supposed to speak concerning their work; they must remain anonymous; and when praise and blame is apportioned, it must fall on the minister who should, in cases of serious error, resign like an officer and gentleman.

Professionality Role- It is an encompassing value that establishes the *modus operandi* of civil services taking into its wake all other values like probity, neutrality, transparency, diligence, punctuality, effectiveness, impartiality, etc. Civil service professionality inculcates values and adopts skills training, continuous learning and education to perform official duties.

Classification in India

Classification of Central Government Posts- The civil service of the Central Government is organized into four groups-

Group 'A' (which includes All India Services), Group 'B',

Group 'C' and

Group 'D'.

If a Service consists of more than one grade, different grades of such service may be included in different groups. The classification serves an important administrative purpose including in matters of recruitment/disciplinary cases, etc. Some allowances are also granted with reference to the classification of the posts. Such classification broadly corresponds to the rank, status and the degree of the level of responsibility attached to the posts. Group 'A' posts carry higher administrative and executive responsibilities and include senior management positions in the Ministries/Departments and field organizations. The middle and junior levels of Group 'A' along with Group 'B' constitute middle management. Group 'C' posts perform supervisory as well as operative tasks and render clerical assistances in Ministries and field organizations. Group 'D' posts are meant for carrying out routine duties. The Central Services (Classification, Control and Appeal) Rules, 1965 provide a concrete and specific criterion for classification of posts in terms of pay.[135]

The Service Concept- An important characteristic of the civil service system at the Centre is its classification based on the concept of the Service. Under this concept, civilian posts are grouped into distinct homogenous cadres under a common Service named on the basis of specific functions attached to the posts in question. The Study Team on Personnel Administration appointed by the Administrative Reforms Commission (1969) appropriately defined a cadre as follows, 'A cadre comprises persons who have been adjudged suitable and recruited to hold a group of positions requiring similar skills - technical, professional and/or administrative; within a Service there may be more than one grade arranged vertically according to the level of responsibility'

Having laid down the working definition of a Service or cadre as above, the Study Team went on to spell out the specific requirements for the constitution of a Service as:

- Determining duties and responsibilities of various positions;
- Translating these in terms of skill requirements;
- Grouping of positions which broadly require similar skills; and
- Gradation of position in terms of responsibilities

According to the Study Team, the concept so developed further presupposes that within a Service, positions at same level are analogous and any member of the service qualified to hold that grade or position can be posted. Thus while constituting a Service, positions are not only examined with reference to skill requirement and are graded but it is also determined whether those positions are also inter-changeable.

A Central Group 'A' Service represents a group of posts belonging to a distinct functional area arranged in a hierarchical order representing different grades or levels of responsibility. All the posts in the Service carry the same functions involving specific skills. They are thus uni-functional. They only differ in rank and status corresponding to given levels of responsibility attached to different grades of posts. The hierarchical arrangement of posts along with the pay scales attached to different grades constitutes what may be called a cadre and the arrangement itself is known as a cadre structure.

There are three All-India Services which are all Group 'A' Services, namely, the Indian Administrative Service, Indian Police Service and Indian Forest Service. These are common to the Centre and the States. The manpower for performing the functions of the Central Government is, however, mainly provided by Central Services and cadres. The Central Group 'A' Services account for the bulk of the Group 'A' posts under the Central Government. They are broadly classified into

- Non-Technical service (Which include audit, income tax, posts, railways)
- Technical Service (which include engineering services),
- Health Services and
- Other Services (which include some engineering and scientific services).[136]

Duty Posts and Reserves- The regular duty posts which constitute the core of the cadre are meant for performing the functions for which the service has been constituted. The reserves are of four types, viz. (i) probationers reserves; (ii) leave reserve; (iii) training reserve; and (iv) deputation reserve.[137]

Recruitment System in India

There are the following services in India

All India Services (AIS) - The members of the AIS serve the government of India and the state government. There are three AIS viz., Indian Administrative Service (IAS), Indian Police Service (IPS) and Indian Forest Service (IFS). The IAS and IPS is of generalist nature for which graduates from any discipline can appear for competitive examination. IAS and IPS are recruited through civil services examination that consists of Preliminary Examination, Main (Written) Examination and Interview Test, conducted by the Union Public Service Commission in accordance with the rules published by the Department of Personnel and Training in the Gazette of India. The IFS is specialist in nature and requires that the aspirants must hold Bachelors degree with at least one of the subjects namely Animal husbandry and Veterinary science, Botany, Chemistry, Geology, Mathematics, Physics, Statistics and Zoology or a Bachelors degree in Agriculture, Forestry or in Engineering. The Union Public Service Commission holds a Screening Test for selection to Indian Forest Service (Main) Examination (Written and Interview), through Civil Services (Preliminary) Examination, in accordance with the Rules published by the Ministry of Environment, Forests and Climate Change in the Gazette of India.

Central Civil Services (CCS) - The members of CCS serves government of India and includes both the generalist and specialist civil services. The members in the generalist services are recruited by civil services examination that consists of Preliminary Examination, Main (Written) Examination and Interview Test, conducted by the Union Public Service Commission in accordance with the rules published by the Department of Personnel and Training in the Gazette of India. Whereas for the specialist recruitment Union Public Service Commission holds a separate examination or Screening Test for selection to specialist service (Main) Examination (Written and Interview), through Civil Services (Preliminary) Examination, in accordance with the rules published by the cadre controlling ministry of the specialist services. The CCS (CCA) Rules, 1965, Schedule Part I and II, Rules 5, 9 (2), 12 (2) and 24 includes following services

Part I - Central Civil Services, Group 'A'.

1. Archaeological Service, Group 'A'.

2. Botanical Survey of India, Group 'A'.

3. Central Engineering (Civil) Group 'A' Service.

4. Central Engineering (Electrical and Mechanical) Group 'A' Service.

5. Central Health Service, Group 'A'.

6. Central Revenues Chemical Service, Group 'A'.

7. Central Secretariat Service-

(a) Selection Grade

(b) Grade- I.

8. General Central Service, Group 'A'

9. Geological Survey of India, Group 'A'.

10. Indian Audit and Accounts Service, Group 'A'.

10-A Indian Civil Accounts Service.

11. Indian Defence Accounts Service

12. Indian Foreign Service, Group 'A'.

13. Indian Meteorological Service, Group 'A'.

14. Indian Postal Service, Group 'A'.

15. Indian Posts &Telegraphs Traffic Service, Group 'A'.

16. Indian Revenue Service –

(a) Customs Branch (Indian Customs Service, Group 'A')

(b) Central Excise Branch (Central Excise Service, Group 'A')

(c) Income Tax Branch (Income Tax Service, Group 'A')

17. Indian Salt Service, Group 'A'.

18. Mercantile Marine Training Ship Service, Group 'A'.

19. Directorate General of Mines Safety, Group 'A'.

20. Overseas Communications Service, Group 'A'.

21. Survey of India, Group 'A'.

22. Indian Telecommunication Service, Group 'A'.

23. Zoological Survey of India, Group 'A'.

24. Indian Frontier Administrative Service, Group 'A'-

(a) Grade I

(b) Grade II

25. Central Legal Service (Grades I, II, III and IV)

26. Railway Inspectorate Service, Group 'A'.

27. Indian Foreign Service, Branch (B) (erstwhile)-

(a) General Cadre, Grade I

(b) General Cadre, Grade II

28. Delhi and Andaman and Nicobar Islands Civil Service, Grade I.

29. Delhi and Andaman and Nicobar Islands Police Service, Grade II.

30. Indian Inspection Service, Group 'A'.

31. Indian Supply Service, Group 'A'.

32. Central Information Service-

(a) Selection Grade

(b) Senior Administrative Grade

(c) Junior Administrative Grade

(d) Grade I

(e) Grade II

33. Indian Statistical Service

34. Indian Economic Service

35. Telegraph Traffic Service, Group 'A'.

36. Central Water Engineering Service, Group 'A'.

37. Central Power Engineering Service, Group 'A'.

38. Company Law Board Service

39. Labour Officers of the Central Pool, Group 'A'.

40. Central Engineering Service (Roads), Group 'A'.

41. Indian Posts and Telegraphs Accounts and Finance Service, Group 'A'.

42. Indian Broadcasting (Engineers) Service

43. Central Trade Service, Group 'A'.

44. Armed Forces Headquarters Civil Services (Group 'A'.)

45. Central Secretariat Official Language Service (Group 'A'.)

Part II - Central Civil Services, Group 'B'.

1. Section Officer Grade of the Central Secretariat Service excluding Section Officers with Group 'A' status.

1-A. Central Secretariat Official Language Service, Group 'B'

2. Assistants' Grade of the Central Secretariat Service

3. Central Secretariat Stenographers' Service, Grade I.

3-A. Central Secretariat Stenographers' Service, Selection Grade

4. Central Secretariat Stenographers' Service, Grade II

5. Central Health Service, Group 'B'

6. India Meteorological Service, Group 'B'

149

6-A. Labour Officers, Group 'B'

7. Postal Superintendents' Service, Group 'B'

8. Postmasters' Service, Group 'B',

9. Telecommunication Engineering Service, Group 'B'

10. Indian Posts and Telegraphs Accounts and Finance Service, Group 'B' Telecommunication Wing

10-A. Indian Posts & Telegraphs Accounts & Finance Service, Postal Wing, Group 'B'

11. Telegraphs Traffic Service, Group 'B'

12. Central Excise Service, Group 'B' – Superintendents, Group 'B' (including Deputy Headquarters Assistant to the Collector) and District Opium Officers, Group 'B'.

13. Customs Appraisers Service, Group 'B'- Principal Appraisers and Head Appraisers

14. Customs Appraisers Service, Group 'B' – Appraisers

15. Customs Preventive Service, Group 'B' – Chief Inspectors

16. Customs Preventive Service, Group 'B' – Inspectors

17. Income Tax Service, Group 'B'

18. Botanical Survey of India, Group 'B'

19. Geological Survey of India, Group 'B'

20. Survey of India, Group 'B'

21. Zoological Survey of India, Group 'B'

22. Central Electrical Engineering Service Group 'B'

23. Central Engineering Service Group 'B'

24. Central Engineering Service, Group 'B':

(i) Posts in the Ministry of Irrigation and Power.

(ii) Posts in the Central Water and Power Commission

(iii) Posts in the Chambal Control Board

(iv) Posts in the Farakka Barrage Control Board

(v) Posts in the Ganga Discharge Circle.

25. Central Power Engineering Service, Group 'B':

(i) Posts in the Ministry of Irrigation and Power

(ii) Posts in the Central Water and Power Commission.

26. Indian Salt Service, Group 'B'

27. Indian Foreign Service (B):

(i) General Cadre Integrated Grades II and III (excluding Section Officers with Group 'A' status).

(ii) Cypher-Sub-Cadre, Grade I

(iii) Stenographers, Sub-cadre, Grade I

(iv) General Cadre, Grade IV

(v) Cypher-Sub-cadre, Grade II

(vi) Stenographers, Sub-cadre, Grade II

28. Delhi and Andaman and Nicobar Islands Civil Service, Grade II

29. Delhi and Andaman and Nicobar Islands Police Service, Grade II

30. Central Information Service, Grades III and IV

31. Central Engineering Service (Roads), Group 'B'

32. General Central Service, Group 'B' –

(i) Post in any Ministry of Department of Government of India, other than the post in respect of which specific provision has been made by a general or special order of the President.

(i-a) Posts outside a Ministry or Department of Government of India, other than the posts in respect of which specific provision has been made by a general or special order of the President

(ii) Posts in Union Territories other than Delhi Administration, the Andaman and Nicobar Islands and the Laccadive, Minicoy and Amindive Islands.

(iii) Delhi Administration – All posts

(iv) The Andaman and Nicobar Islands – All posts

(v) The Lakshadweep Administration – All posts

33. All Group 'B' posts of the Departmentalized Accounts Offices of the Government of India

Part III - Central Civil Services, Group 'C'.

1. Central Secretariat Clerical Service, Upper Division and Lower Division Grade

1-A. Central Secretariat Stenographers' Service, Grade III

2. Posts and Telegraphs Accountants Service: Senior and Junior Accountants

3. Indian Foreign Service (B): General Cadre, Grade V and VI

4. General Central Service, Group 'C'

(i) Posts in the Ministry/ Department of Government other than the posts in respect of which specific provision has been made by a general or special order of the President.

(ii) Posts in non-Secretariat Office other than posts in respect of which specific provision has been made by a general or special order of the President.

(iii) Posts in Union Territories

(iv) All Group 'C' posts of the Departmentalized Accounts Offices of the Government of India.

5. Central Secretariat Official Language Service, Group 'C'

Part IV - Central Civil Services, Group 'D'.

1. General Central Service, Group 'D'

(i) Posts in Ministries or Departments of Government other than posts in respect of which specific provision has been made by a general or special order of the president.

(ii) Posts in non-Secretariat Offices other than posts in respect of which specific provision has been made by a general or special order of the President

(iii) Posts in Union Territories

(iv) All Group 'D' posts of the Departmentalized Accounts Offices of the Government of India

State Civil Services- The members of State Civil Service serves the state government and includes both the generalist and specialist civil services. The members in the generalist services are recruited by state civil services examination that consists of preliminary examination, main (written) examination and interview test, conducted by the union/state public service commission. Whereas for the specialist recruitment union/state public service commission holds a separate examination or makes certain educational qualification as a condition for specialist service in the state civil service examination itself.

Training in India- Agencies and Institutions

History of Civil Service Training- On 23 October 1805, "Hailey Bury House near Hertford" and its surrounding 60-acre estate were purchased by the Directors of the East India Company for the site of their proposed East India College. The Company's aim was to build a college to educate civil servants to work in India with the mission to "qualify them for governing themselves." The East India College had a specific mission. In the past, its administrators had been largely employed to oversee commercial transactions. By the late eighteenth century, they had become increasingly involved in the legal and fiscal administration of, and providing the government to, millions of people of various languages, manners, customs and religions. By 1800, a system which had also been based significantly on patronage was ill-equipped for the new world. The East India College was set up to provide a thorough training environment for all new civil servants in India and to ensure that no such official should go to India until he was at least 18. From 1806 to 1857, the East India College thrived at Haileybury, training more than 2,000 pupils for a future in the administration of the Indian subcontinent. The depth and breadth of subjects taught were seen as crucial to the effective education of this new generation of "writers", as they were known. Lessons offered a broad but detailed curriculum designed best to equip each new pupil for their future careers. Subjects taught included political economy and history, mathematics and natural philosophy, classics, law and humanity and philology. Crucially, languages played a significant part in the curriculum and included Hindustani, Sanskrit, Telugu and Persian. Despite its grand beginnings and early promise, the East India College was on borrowed time; the East India Company itself was seen as being too powerful for its own good. By the mid 1850s, there was a movement in the land against patronage and a greater desire to see open competition and reward by meritocracy. It was also now felt that students leaving Universities in Great Britain should have equal opportunity to serve in India rather than have to be channeled through the College. So, on July 16th, 1855 an Act of Parliament was passed "to relieve the East India Company from the obligation to maintain the College at Haileybury" and the first open competitive examinations for service in India were held at King's College, London in the same year. The East India College closed its doors, seemingly for good, on 31st January 1858.[138] After the introduction of merit in the recruitment for civil services examination, the successful candidates underwent one or two year's probation in England, this period was spent at the University of Oxford, the University of Cambridge, the School of Oriental Studies in London or Trinity College, Dublin, where a candidate studied the law and institutions of India, including criminal law and the Law of Evidence, which together gave knowledge of the revenue system, as well as reading Indian history and learning the language of the Province to which they had been assigned.[139]

Lal Bahadur Shastri National Academy of Administration (LBSNAA), Mussoorie[140]

On April 15, 1958 the then Home Minister announced in the Lok Sabha a proposal to set up a National Academy of Administration, where training would be given to all the recruits of the Civil Services. On 13th April, 1959 the first batch of 115 officers started training in Metcalfe House. The Ministry of Home Affairs decided to amalgamate the IAS Training School, Delhi and the IAS Staff College, Shimla to form a National Academy of Administration at Mussoorie. The

Academy was set up in 1959 and was called the 'National Academy of Administration'. Its status was that of an 'attached office' of the Government of India under the Ministry of Home Affairs. In October 1972, its name was changed to "Lal Bahadur Shastri Academy of Administration" and in July 1973, the word "National" was added and the Academy is now known as the "Lal Bahadur Shastri National Academy of Administration". The prestigious "Charleville Hotel" built around 1870, provided the location and initial infrastructure for the Academy. There have been subsequent expansions and several new buildings have been constructed and others acquired over the years.

The Lal Bahadur Shastri National Academy of Administration (LBSNAA), Mussoorie is the premier training institution for the higher civil services in India. A common Foundation Course is held for entrants to All India Services and all Group 'A' services of the Union. The professional training to regular recruits of the Indian Administrative Service (IAS) and members of the Royal Bhutan Service is conducted after the Foundation Course. The Academy also conducts in-service and Mid-Career Training Programme (MCTP) for members of the IAS and Induction Training Programme for officers promoted to the IAS from State Civil Services, as well as workshops and seminars on policy issues.

The Training Programmes- The Academy Offers variety programmes, all of which have been developed based on a detailed training needs assessment:

Foundation Course (15 weeks)- The Academy stands out as one of the very few institutions in the world with focus not only on Civil Services capacity building but also inter-services camaraderie and cooperation.

This Course is intended for the new recruits to the All India Services and Central Services (Group A). It equips fresh entrants with requisite skills, knowledge and attitude to shoulder responsibility as public servants. Their main objectives are:

- to foster greater cooperation and coordination among various public services by building an esprit de corps;
- to promote all round development of the personality of an officer trainee- intellectual, moral, physical and aesthetic.

IAS Professional Course Phase-I (26 weeks)-This Course imparts rigorous training to the Officer Trainee of the Indian Administrative Services in a wide range of subjects to enable them to handle varied assignments that they would typically hold in the first decade of their service. This programme has two basic modules: the Winter-study tour and academic module.

The Winter Study Tour (WST) precedes the academic module wherein the Officers Training travels across the country to experience its rich cultural diversity. It's also includes a week-long attachment with the Bureau of Parliamentary Studies which exposes them to the functioning of the Parliamentary system in India. The Officer Trainees also call on important dignitaries such as the President of India, the Vice-President of India, the Prime Minister of India and others during this attachment.

The Academy module is theme-based. It covers the following subjects:

- IAS in perspective/Role of the IAS in policy making
- National Security/ Law and order.
- Agriculture /Land Management and Administration
- Rural Development /Decentralization and Panchayati Raj
- Urban management/Infrastructure and Public-Private Partnership
- E-Governance/Office Management/Administrative Skills
- Soft skills (Leadership, Organizational Behaviour, Inter-personal skills)
- Projects Management, Engineering Skills and ICIT
- Financial management and project Appraisal
- Social Sector/Weaker Section & Minorities

District Training (52 weeks) - One year of district training, in effect, is a drill to enable the Officers Trainee to see, study and live the paradox that is the quintessential India- with its unfathomable diversity, myriad challenges and opportunities. They study the administrative setup, interact with people, their representatives and officials in order to understand the paradigm of development as well as effectiveness of strategies.

IAS Professional Course Phase- II (6 weeks)- This phase of induction level training provides the officer Trainees with a platform to share individual learning experiences gained in the field and enables them to articulate the strengths and weaknesses of our administration and governance. This phase of interactive learning is supplemented with special sessions with distinguished experts from within and outside the Government. The penultimate phase of training serves as a vibrant learning ground before the Officer Trainees launch their career in public service.

Mid- Career Training Programmes- The Mid Career Training Programme was initiated in 2007 with the aim of imparting structured in-service training to IAS officers to prepare them for higher levels of responsibilities, spanning three phases, viz. Phase-III, Phase-IV and Phase-V training programmes. The programme was initially outsourced to various national/ international institutions for a period of three

160

years. Since 2010, the Academy has been mandated the responsibility of designing and delivering each of these courses.

Phase-III- To equip officers who have completed seven to nine years of service for effective transition to strategy formulation and its implementation.

Objectives

- To appreciate contemporary developments in political economy at the national and global level

- To equip officers with tools, skills and knowledge that will help them achieve 'excellence in implementation' of programs.

- To design and implement BPR in Government and leveraging IT to improve public service delivery

- To strengthen communication, inter-personal and team-building skills and appreciate the centrality of values in governance.

Phase-IV- To equip officers who have completed fifteen to sixteen years of service for effective transition to policy formulation and better implementation.

Objectives

- Appreciate contemporary developments in political economy at the global and national level,

- Understand the process of public policy formulation, analysis and evaluation,
- Enhance domain knowledge in the context of public policy,
- Strengthen leadership and negotiation skills, and,
- Appreciate the centrality of values in governance.

Phase-V- To equip officers who have completed twenty-six to twenty-eight years of service for effective transition to strategy formulation and its implementation.

Objectives

- Develop a wider global and national perspective in order to formulate strategies to meet future challenges
- Understand the importance of inter-sectoral policy design and implementation
- Provide effective leadership in her work environment
- Reinforce service networks essential for policy formulation and implementation

Induction Training Program (6 weeks) - The Induction Training Programme is conducted for officers promoted to the IAS from the state civil services. The aim of the course is to update levels of knowledge, skills and to provide opportunities for exchange of ideas, views and experiences with people who have developed expertise in different sectors of national development. Considerable focus is given to new managerial techniques and skills as well as to frontier areas of technology and its management. The course aims to impart an all India perspective to the officers promoted to the IAS.

Objectives

- To acquire & update interdisciplinary knowledge & skills to function effectively as administrators.

- To acquire a pan Indian perspective on administrative issues and govern- ance challenges through exchange of experiences, ideas & views.

- To equip the participants with new Information Communication Technology skills and managerial techniques.

Sardar Vallabhbhai Patel National Police Academy (SVPNPA), Hyderabad

The Academy started functioning on 15th Sept, 1948 at Mount Abu, Rajasthan and moved to Hyderabad, Andhra Pradesh in the year 1975. The National Police Academy (NPA), trains officers of the Indian Police Service. The following courses are conducted by the academy.

- Basic Training Course- for IPS officers;

- Compulsory Mid Career Training Programme- for officers of SP, DIG, and IG/Additional DG levels of the Indian Police Service;

- Training of Trainers' Courses- for the trainers of various police training institutions in the country;

- IPS Induction Training Course- for State Police Service Officers; and

- Short specialized thematic Courses, Seminars and Workshops on professional subjects for all levels of police officers

Foreign police officers and other officers belonging to Army/IAS/IFS/Judiciary, Public Sector Undertakings, Nationalized Banks, Insurance Companies etc. also attend various specialized courses conducted by the academy. The Academy is affiliated to Osmania University for conducting courses on police subjects for IPS officers.[141]

Administrative Staff College of India (ASCI), Hyderabad

Established in 1956 and modeled on Henley-on-Thames College, England. At the initiative of the government and the corporate sector, the ASCI, has pioneered post-experience management education in India. ASCI equips corporate managers, administrators, entrepreneurs and academicians with the skills to synthesize managerial theory and practice; and respond to the ever-increasing complexity of managerial issues confronting government, industrial enterprises and non-government organizations.[142]

The National Institute of Rural Development & Panchayati Raj (NIRD &PR), Hyderabad

NIRD is an autonomous organization under the Union Ministry of Rural Development, is a premier national centre of excellence in rural development. Recognized internationally as one of the UN-ESCAP Centres of Excellence in HRD, it builds capacities of rural development functionaries, elected representatives, academicians and young students through inter-related activities of training, research and consultancy. Originally established as National Institute of Community Development in 1958, the Institute shifted to its Hyderabad Campus in 1965 and renamed as National Institute of Rural Development in 1977. Its objectives are

- Organize training programmes, conferences, seminars and workshops for senior level development managers, elected representatives, bankers, NGOs and other stakeholders;

- Undertake aid, promote and coordinate research;

- Study the functioning of the Panchayati Raj Institutions (PRIs) and rural development programmes across the states;

- Analyze and propose solutions to problems in planning and implementation of the programmes for rural development; and

- Develop content and disseminate information through periodicals, reports, e-modules and other publications

Training play a pivoted role in capacity building of functionaries involved in rural development. The NIRD has expertise and excellent infrastructure to train senior and middle level development functionaries engaged in policy formulation, management and implementation of rural development programmes. The training and teaching programmes are intended to create knowledge base, develop skills and infuse right attitudes and values. About 1000 programmes are offered every year. Besides, the Institute conducts several international training programmes sponsored by the Ministry of External Affairs and the Ministry of Rural Development. Participants from several Afro-Asian countries undergo training at NIRD every year. About 28,000 trainees pass through the portals of NIRD annually.[143]

Foreign Service Institute (FSI), New Delhi[144]

The FSI was established in 1986 by the Government of India primarily to cater to the professional training needs of the Indian Foreign Service and the Ministry of External Affairs. FSI has diversified its activities to include courses for foreign diplomats in its efforts at building bridges of friendship and cooperation with countries around the world, as well as other Indian government services. Though the Foreign Service Institute started functioning in 1986, the training of Indian Foreign Service officers began with an October 1946 Cabinet decision which stated that "The special knowledge and the professional skill required of a diplomat can only be acquired through careful training."

Initially, the Indian Foreign Service (IFS) officer training consisted of a three-month preliminary course in Delhi followed by 18 months in foreign universities, with students under the general supervision of the Indian representative in the country concerned, followed by one year of training at headquarters in India.

The Cabinet approved the proposal to establish the Foreign Service Training Institute on December 20, 1983. The training institute was intended to train not only the new recruits, but also mid-career officers. In 1993, the Foreign Service Training Institute (FSTI) was renamed as the Foreign Service Institute (FSI). FSI is headed by the Dean, a senior Foreign Service officer of the rank of Secretary in the Ministry of External Affairs. It also has two Joint Secretary-level officers.

Program for Officer Trainees- The total training period for Probationers in India – LBSNAA, Mussoorie, and FSI New Delhi, desk and field attachments should not exceed a total of 15 months. In principle, the time distribution would be:

(i) LBSNAA, Mussoorie (3 months);

(ii) FSI – First Phase (5 months);

(iii) On the job training with the desks of MEA (2 months): (iv) Field attachments, namely, District, Army, Bharat Darshan, Mission Attachment, etc. (3 months);

(v) FSI – Second Phase (1 month); and followed by

(vi) Pre-departure attachment with the concerned Territorial Division, including brief attachment with other relevant line Ministries (1 month).

The purpose of the training programme for probationers should be to expose them to the basics of all the aspects of India's foreign policy; relevant domestic issues; management/housekeeping tools; diplomatic skills, diaspora and consular issues and other aspects including conversation, writing, negotiations and public speaking skills.

MCTP Phase I - This training fills the knowledge gaps in core functional areas as well as in essential management disciplines. It facilitates the transition of officers from Analyst to Integrator, Tactician to Strategist, Bricklayer to Architect, Problem Solver to Agenda Setter and Supporting Cast Member to Lead Role. The duration is for four weeks and is for IFS officers with 5-8 years of service.

MCTP Phase II- This training accelerates the transition of an officer from functional specialist to strategic leader. MCTP II addresses the core needs of catching up with emerging foreign policy issues by providing some domain specialization, exposure to domestic issues of relevance and modern management tools for developing leadership skills. The duration is for three weeks distributed at (i) FSI; and (ii) premier international institutions. This course is mandatory for officers of Gr. IV of IFS (Director Level)

MCTP Phase II- This is an existing mandatory phase of MCTP for officers of Gr. III of IFS (Joint Secretary level). The national/international institutions are co-opted for dealing with some of the modules with specialized domain expertise.

Training Capsules for IFS (B) - It includes capsule programs on basic computer course, Account, Integrated Missions Accounting System (IMAS), Trade promotion, PROTOCOL, Consular manners, Passport, Visa, Office procedure, and financial procedure.

Other Training Courses

- Professional Course for Foreign Diplomats
- Special Course for ASEAN Diplomats
- Special Course for Indian Ocean Rim Association for Regional Cooperation (IORARC)
- Special Course for Other Developing Countries

Indira Gandhi National Forest Academy, Dehradun[145]

The beginning of formal training of IFS officers dates back to 1867 when five candidates were selected to undergo training in France and Germany. This continued up to 1885 except for a short break on account of war between France and Russia. From 1885 to 1905, the training of IFS Probationers was organized at Cooper's Hill, London where 173 Officers were trained. The training of IFS Probationers between 1895 and 1927 was held in Universities of Oxford, Cambridge and Edinburgh. In 1920, the Government of India took the historic decision that the IFS Probationers may be trained at one centre and consequent to the establishment of Forest Research Institute at Dehradun, the training started in India in 1926. It continued up to 1932, when due to lack of demand for officers, it had to be discontinued.

The Government of India Act of 1935, which transferred forestry to Provisional list, resulted in abolition of the IFS training. With the retirement of IFS officers, the demand for trained foresters cropped up and thus Indian Forest College was born in 1938. The Superior Forest Service officers, recruited from different states, were trained in IFC thus retaining the all India character of the service.

The management of the forest went into the hands of the provincial government in 1935 and even today the Forest Departments are managing the forest of the country under the respective State governments. Since the subject of forestry was shifted to the concurrent list in the year 1977, the central government plays an important role, particularly at the policy level in the management of the forest.

IFS Probationers' Training Course- IFS officers of the country are part of the nation's management expertise pool. The training course for the IFS Probationers is designed to address these requirements. Some of the essential elements of the training are as follows:

- Capacity building by imparting technical knowledge and skills required in forestry sector
- Enhancing management skills
- The personality development as a member of Indian Forest Service

To achieve the above course objectives, training at the Academy extends over a period of 2 years. Comprehensive exposures to all the subjects that are directly or indirectly related to forestry are provided. The course is designed to be covered in phases as under

- Foundation Course
- Professional Phase I
- Professional Phase II
- Convocation Phase

The probation period in IFS extends over two years. After successful completion of probation (which includes successful completion of training at LBSNAA and IGNFA), an Officer is given posting as Assistant Conservator of Forests on his joining in the State Cadre. On the basis of sound service record and successful completion of probation in all respects, the Officer is confirmed in the service. Thereafter, depending upon the availability of posts, he is appointed in the senior time scale of the IFS as Deputy Conservator of Forests.

Skill Up-gradation Training Programme- The Skill Up-gradation Training Programme is imparted in the Academy to officers inducted into IFS from SFS since September 1996. This is done to give an All India perspective of the service and update the knowledge and skill of the officers.

Other Trainings- The other training includes

- Joint training programme of IAS/IPS/IFS
- Sensitisation programme for other stakeholders

National Academy of Customs, Excise and Narcotics (NACEN), New Delhi

The NACEN is the apex institute of Government of India for capacity building in the field of indirect taxation. It also plays a vital role in international capacity building by imparting training to officers of various countries in the field of customs, drug laws and environment protection. The NACEN undertakes probation training, In-Service Training, International Cooperation and Training, and Mid Career Training Program[146]

National Academy of Direct Taxes (NADT), Nagpur

The first training course was held at the Income Tax Office at Queen's Road, Bombay. The residential accommodation of the probationers was popularly known as Bhootkhana. Some Income Tax officers took upon themselves the responsibility of training the newly recruited officers. The training set up was shifted to Kolkata in 1950 for administrative reasons. In 1957, the training of directly recruited IRS officers was shifted to Nagpur. The probationers arrived in mid-November from the National Academy of Administration, Mussoorie. In their first spell of training, the probationers were mainly provided with theoretical inputs. Classes were conducted up to middle of March, when the first departmental examination was held. The Director of Inspection IT declared results for the first departmental exams in early June. The second spell of training ended by mid-September. In this phase, equal emphasis was given to theoretical and practical aspects of Income Tax. The second departmental exams were usually held in September. The Director of Inspection IT declared results of the examination in early December. After the second departmental examination, talks were given on the Finance Act of the year. The officers were briefed on the working of Income Tax Offices across the country. Probationers visited the local Income Tax offices to get a feel of the ground reality. By mid-

November, the probationers left for a three week long Bharat Darshan. Valediction of the outgoing batch and the inauguration of the new batch were held simultaneously in December every year. The courses at NADT includes Induction Training, In Service Training, International Training, Foundation Training, Outreach, and orientation.[147]

The National Academy of Audit and Accounts (NAAA), Shimla

The (NAAA) is the apex training institute of the Indian Audit & Accounts Department (IA&AD). The training school started in Madras in 1949. The IA&AS training school was set up at Chadwick house in Shimla in year 1950 but it shifted back to Madras in 1953 and from 1957 it is in Shimla. It provides Induction training, Orientation training, In Service training and also undertakes international engagements.[148]

Training for Various Railway Services

The railway service in India is one of the largest networks of railways in the world. The railway department is the only department whose budget is separately presented than the general budget by the government. The training needs of the various railways services in India are provided by different Railway Training Institutions. The training institutions of various railway services in India and their locations are

Service	Training Institution
Indian Railway Service of Engineers (IRSE)	Indian Railway Institute of Civil Engineering (IRICEN), Pune
Indian Railway Service of Mechanical Engineers (IRSME)	Indian Railways Institute of Mechanical and Electrical Engineering (IRIMEE), Jamalpur
Indian Railway Service of Electrical Engineers (IRSEE)	Indian Railways Institute of Electrical Engineering (IRIEEN), Nasik
Indian Railway Service of Signal Engineers (IRSSE)	The Indian Railway Institute of Signal Engineering and Telecommunication (IRISET), Secunderabad
The Indian Railways Stores Service (IRSS)	Railway Staff College, Vadodara
The Indian Railway Traffic Service (IRTS)	Indian Railways Institute of Transport Management, Lucknow
The Indian Railway Accounts Service (IRAS)	Railway Staff College, Vadodara
The Indian Railway Personnel Service (IRPS)	Railway Staff College, Vadodara
Railway Protection Force (RPF)	Jagjivan Ram RPF Academy, Lucknow

Indian Economic Service- Direct recruits joining the service, after being offered appointment, undergo a comprehensive probationary training comprising the Foundation course (conducted for the All India Services and the Central Civil Services), training on Economics at the Institute of Economic

175

Growth, Delhi, and training/ attachment at various national level Institutes of repute across the country (Indian Statistical Institute, Indian School of Business, etc). Capacity building of serving officers is carried out on an ongoing basis by conducting various in-service training programmes suited to the officers' needs, from the point of view of building up professional capacity at work as well as developing soft skills. The flagship in-service training programme is the mid-career training of six-week duration comprising domestic learning and foreign learning components, conducted at a reputed management Institute in the country. Officers of the service are required to participate in three such mid-career training courses at different phases in their career.[149]

Indian Institute of Public Administration (IIPA), New Delhi[150]

Pandit Jawaharlal Nehru when he established the Indian Institute of Public Administration on March 29, 1954 based on the recommendations of a survey carried out in 1953 by Prof. Paul H. Appleby, Dean, Maxwell School of Citizenship and Public Affairs, Syracuse University and a Consultant with the Ford Foundation invited to advice on the subject, by the Government of India.

Training and Educational Programmes- The Institute conducts around 90-100 short and long-term learning programmes aimed at capacity enhancement of civil servants, defence officers, technocrats and executives of public sector undertakings (PSUs) currently. These programmes are either fee-based or sponsored by the Government. It designs customised programmes for other organisations. Its flagship training initiatives include a ten-month Advanced Professional Programme in Public Administration (APPPA) that is sponsored by Department of Personnel and Training (DoPT). This multi-faceted programme for senior officers of the Central Government was started in 1975 and is now in its 39th year. The Institute nurtures close academic association with universities, research centres, training institutions and government departments. Another important sponsorship is the series of managerial skill-development engagements for senior scientists supported by the Department of Science and Technology. Customised programmes for private sector industry especially in areas of their interface with Government at all levels and activating knowledge centres in Ministries and State Governments are new initiatives. The Institute also organises a number of international training programmes for participants from developing and developed. Apart from training the IIPA undertakes-

- Research
- Policy Advice

- Conferences/Workshops/Seminars
- Dissemination of Information

Promotion in India

In India for the first time, the East India Company accepted the seniority principle for promotion in year 1669. The Charter Act, 1793 continued with it. Further with time as merit principle was established for recruitment, the Indian Civil Service Act 1861 established Indian Civil Service and then on the formula of merit cum seniority was fallowed with the relative weightage shifting from service to service. The pay commission and administrative reforms commission have made various observations and recommendations from time to time in this regard.

Article 309 of Indian Constitution states that, "recruitment and conditions of service of persons serving the Union or a State Subject to the provisions of this Constitution, Acts of the appropriate Legislature may regulate the recruitment, and conditions of service of persons appointed, to public services and posts in connection with the affairs of the Union or of any State: Provided that it shall be competent for the President or such person as he may direct in the case of services and posts in connection with the affairs of the Union, and for the Governor of a State or such person as he may direct in the case of services and posts in connection with the affairs of the State, to make rules regulating the recruitment, and the conditions of service of persons appointed, to such services and posts until provision in that behalf is made by or under an Act of the appropriate Legislature under this article, and any rules so made shall have effect subject to the provisions of any such Act"

For an impartial and uniform procedure of recruitment to services, it is necessary that there should be prescribed recruitment rules for every post/grade and all recruitment made in accordance with these rules. In deciding on the methods of recruitment the main consideration naturally is whether a direct recruit or a person with experience of work in the next lower grade would be more suitable for appointment to the post/grade. Not infrequently departmental experience in an office is not only essential but may also be preferable to mere academic qualifications for maintaining efficiency. It is also natural for, persons serving in the lower grades to look forward to promotion to highest posts in which their experience can be used with advantage to the State. For these reasons, promotion is one important methods of recruitment to various services and posts under the Central Government.[151]

Principles for promotion- The Guiding tenets followed in India are as follows:

(i) Every person eligible for promotion and in the field of choice should be considered for promotion.

(ii) It is desirable that —

(a) Standard for promotion should be strictly adhered to. Where prescribed standards are considered too rigorous to meet practical requirements, they may be reviewed in consultation with the UPSC/Departmental Promotion Committee (DPC).

(b) Minimum length of service in the lower grade prescribed as a condition for promotion to the higher grade is not materially different from that prescribed by other departments for promotion to similar grades involving the same nature of duties and responsibilities.[152]

(iii) Employing Departments' should estimate the number of vacancies which might arise in the succeeding year for being filled by promotion on the recommendation of a DPC and also convene the meeting of the DPC at regular annual intervals.[153]

(iv) The administrative authorities should ensure that the information furnished to Departmental Promotion Committees is accurate and in proper order in all respects. Ministries may investigate all cases of delay and submission of incorrect particulars to the DPC and take suitable action against the persons responsible for default.[154]

(v) If a candidate who is recommended for direct recruitment is also among those recommended for promotion by the DPC, he should be appointed as a direct recruit or a promotee according as his turn for appointment comes earlier from direct recruitment list or from the promotion list.[155]

(vi) Officiating appointments to the higher grade, of whatever duration should, as far as possible, be made in the order in which names appear in the select list. Exceptions to this rule may become necessary where a number of vacancies are to be filled within a comparatively short period and it is convenient and desirable to make postings with due regard to the location and experience of the officers concerned or short term vacancies have to be filled on a local and ad hoc basis. An out of turn promotion in such circumstances should not, however, give the officer concerned any superior claim in the matter of seniority, or confirmation, which should be determined on the basis of the order of select list.[156]

Performance Appraisal in India

The system of writing Annual Confidential Reports (ACRs), for the All India Services governed by the All India Services (Confidential Roll) Rules 1970 is replaced by All India Services (Performance Appraisal Report) Rules, 2007.

- A comprehensive performance appraisal dossier is maintained which consist of the specified documents.
- The reporting authority write the performance appraisal report in specified form as may be specified and the officer

reported upon and the reporting, reviewing and accepting authority ensures that the portions of the forms which are to be filled in by them are completed by them within the time limit

- A performance appraisal report assessing the performance, character, conduct and qualities of every member of the Service is written for each financial year (to be recorded by 31st December) or as may be specified by the Government.

- A certified true copy of the performance appraisal report is sent to the Central Government or the State Government or both as is applicable.

- The full annual performance appraisal report, including the overall grade and assessment of integrity, shall be disclosed to the officer reported upon after finalization by the accepting authority to enable the officer reported upon to represent his case.

- The officer reported upon may have the option to give his comments (restricted to in terms of attributes, work output and competency) on the performance appraisal report in writing to the accepting authority within fifteen days of the receipt of the Performance Appraisal Report.

- The accepting authority shall consider the comments of the officer reported upon, the views of the reporting authority and the reviewing authority and after due consideration may accept them and modify the performance appraisal report accordingly and the decision and final grading shall be communicated to the officer reported upon within fifteen days of receipt of the views of the reviewing authority.

- In case the officer reported upon chooses to represent against the final assessment conveyed to him according to this procedure, he may represent his case through the accepting authority for a decision by the Referral Board, as specified in the Schedule 3 of the All India Services (Performance Appraisal Report) Rules, 2007, within one month, provided that such representation shall be confined to errors of facts.

- The Referral Board shall consider the representation of the officer reported upon in the light of the comments of the reporting authority, the reviewing authority and the accepting authority and confirm or modify the performance appraisal report, including the overall grade and the decision of the Referral Board shall be confined only to errors of facts and the decision of the Referral Board shall be final.

- In case an entry or assessment is upgraded or downgraded, reasons for the same shall be recorded in the performance appraisal report.

- The entire performance appraisal report, including the overall grade, shall thereafter be communicated to the officer reported upon which shall conclude the process of assessment and no further representation of any kind shall be entertained thereafter.

- Nothing in the rules shall be deemed to preclude an officer from making a memorial to the President on the Performance Appraisal Report, as provided under rule 25 of the All India Services (Discipline and Appeal) Rules, 1969.

Review of the Performance Appraisal Report for All India Services[157] This review is prompted by the widespread dissatisfaction with the working of the PAR system at all levels. There is a perception that the attempts to quantify and bring objectivity have not been successful, even though the current system of Performance Appraisal Report (PAR) is laid down in the All India Service (PAR) Rules in 2007. The main problems and the proposed solutions are summarized below.

Problems- The main problems categorized as conceptual and procedural are as follows

- Conceptual Flaws
    1. Lack of prioritization
    2. Poor Definitions of Standard Terms
    3. No Ex-Ante Agreement on Deviations from the Targets
    4. Deceptive Façade of Quantification
    5. No Ex-Ante Agreement on Definition
    6. Emphasis on Personality rather than Results

7. Lack of Linkage between Individual and Organizational Performance
- Procedural Flaws
    1. PARs are filled in Ex-Post
    2. Lack of Proper Training
    3. Lack of discipline in adhering to deadlines

Proposed Reforms- The proposed reforms includes the following measures.

1. Change the Structure of Section Dealing with Results (Tasks and Deliverables)

   The proposed methodology for the Performance Measurement System consists of seven steps and is consistent with the methodology for Results-Framework Documents.

2. Reduce the Weight for Personal Qualities and Functional Skills

   The relative weight for Results-Framework should be 80% and the balance of 20% should be assigned to Personal Qualities and Functional Skills. Here too, there should be a very clear understanding of what is being measured and how it is being measured. In other words, we must reduce outright subjectivity to a minimum.

3. Use more Rigorous Instruments for Assessing Personal Qualities and Functional Skills

4. Use only the Results Framework for Performance Related Incentives
5. Make Departmental Results-Framework Documents a Pre-Requisite for PAR
6. Make the PAR Process Paperless
7. Require Attendance in a Mandatory 2-Week Training Program
8. Develop a Multimedia Self-Help Toolkit for PAR

GENERALISTS AND SPECIALISTS

Meaning of Generalists

It is concerned with the managerial process of public administration that involves planning, staffing, coordinating, command, control, etc. The general educational competence normally determined by university degree from any faculty is required as qualifying conditions to enter in administrative services is referred as generalist administration. The positive connotation of 'generalist' is professional administrator.

The Generalist means mature administrators, who had education in linguistics or classics and is a highly intelligent gentleman with a liberal education augmented by certain personal qualities of character, poise and leadership, good intuitive judgment, right feelings and a broad background rather than narrowly specialized knowledge and skills.[158]

Generalists are experienced administrators or career executives who can undertake flexible assignments, render proper administrative and policy opinion.

One usage considers a person as a generalist who is known by the amount of administrative work actually performed compared with specialist duties. When a specialist performs administrative duties either in the higher hierarchies or don't use special knowledge than the specialist turn out to be generalist. Generalists are super-bureaucrats with a broader and long term perspective.

As one move up the hierarchical career ladder the nature of works becomes generalist, the policy making, direction nature of job remains same in almost all technical and non technical departments. The higher responsibilities demands from generalist sound mental poise, broad vision and wisdom garner from the experiences of career life. That helps to have a comprehensive, integrated approach.

Role of Generalist in Administration

- Policy making
- Policy implementation
- Integrate diverse and myriad view and perspectives.
- Advisory role
- Problem solving

Meaning of Specialists

Administrators who have special knowledge about a particular subject are specialists. They are recruited by the process that demands special qualification as a condition for recruitment. The 'subject matter view' of public administration holds that only knowledge and proficiency in managerial functions is not enough for public administration but the growing complexity and specialization demand special knowledge for effective and efficient public administration. Special qualification, which normally is a graduation with certain subjects that is what, is required as the qualification condition for certain services, and the administrators of such services are known as specialists. The characteristic of specialists includes aptitude about discipline, passion for subject, sustained commitment, professionalism and pursuit for specialization.

Role of Specialists in Administration

- domain knowledge for complex and technical working
- In public administration where subject matters, specialists are vital.
- Important role in specialized areas of policy and decision making.
- Role in traditional public administration and also in emerging sphere.

Prototypes[159]

The 'specialists v/s generalists formulation is basically a logically fallacy, it was very well analyzed by Yehezkel Dror who states that, it reduces a multiplicity of attributes into two patterns, assuming there is some necessary internal relationship which excludes (or, at least, reduces the probability of) other combinations. Dror elaborates this point little further by, trying to break down the 'specialist' and 'generalist' prototypes into components, which identify four categories of characteristics, each one of which includes a number of dimensions, as illustrated in Table.

Some Components of 'Specialists/Generalists' Prototype

Categories	Dimension of Each Category
Academic Knowledge	none…much; narrow…broad; monographic…nonographic; substantive (by areas)…methodological (by areas)
Personal Qualities	closed minded…open minded; non creative…highly creative; rigid…elastic; detail oriented…general picture oriented
Experience	high level…low level; one area…multiple areas; center…field
Tactic capacities	Good…bad human relations (in different situations); good…bad intuitive judgment in few… many areas; good…bad managerial talents (in different types of organization)

It may well be that a hundred years ago, and perhaps also fifty years ago, the class structure of a country in combination with its educational system and the structure of academic disciplines did, in fact, create a few clusters of these various attributes: Thus, in England, academic training at Cambridge and Oxford in classics or mathematics often went together with an open mind, a broad view, elasticity, good intuitive judgement, broad experience, and similar features of the ideal generalist. But this was not the result of a direct causal relationship between the attributes (studying the classics resulting in an open mind, etc.), but rather of other variables (e.g., persons with an open mind tending to study the classics). Even less is there reason to assume an exclusive causal relationship, such as only studying the classics can result in an open mind, and so on. It may well be that - all other things being equal - some contemporary methods of teaching economics (but not all) tend to result in narrow-minded experts fulfilling many of the negative expectations of the 'anti-expert' school. Yehezkel Dror's only claim is that this is not necessarily so. A revised curriculum in economics can combine rigorous training of the mind with encouraging creativity and education in taking a broad 'systems view' of social problems. The changes in student interests and in socio-economic origin of students, the changes in the structure of knowledge and in methods of teaching, and the changes in the public service itself - all these combine to add to the logical fallacies of the 'experts vs. professionals' formulation an even more important behavioral refutation. Pluralistic character of modern public administration, increasing needs both top-level scientific and experience-based knowledge and top-quality judgment and moral values.

Conventional thinking on the 'experts vs. generalists' formulation already recognized that it was a problem not of one or the other, but of the proper relation between them but the required qualities of public administration cannot be achieved by any mixture of 'experts and generalists' in the traditional sense. This dichotomy needs to be overcome not only in discourse, but in action, to achieve the public administration qualities needed for handling new and difficult problems and for absorbing new very promising and very frightening knowledge under conditions of accelerated social change.

Models of Relationship

The nature of relationship between the generalists and the specialists has varied in different countries depending on models adopted for their inter relationship the four types of hierarchies observed in this context are as fallows.

- Separate Hierarchy - Under this system there is common pay for generalists and the specialists but greater respect for latter

- Parallel Hierarchy - Both have their own respective hierarchies and they work together in a coordinated manner.

- Joint Hierarchy - The generalist and specialist report jointly to their common generalist superior likewise a minister may also be advised by the generalist as well as by the specialist.

- Unified Hierarchy - Such a system assumes and envisages the existence of a unified civil service under which all the services and cadres are merged in an integrated service. Accordingly each of the existing services gets converted into a functional branch of the single unified service retaining its separate professional distinctiveness the formal structure of civil service in Pakistan, since 1973 has been an this pattern. Experience however shows that it is difficult to radically eliminate the culture of stratification even in a unified civil service.

This is not exhaustive list of models of juxtaposing the respective roles of generalist and the specialists. Moreover, an actual pattern may not fit totally into any of the above four hierarchies.

NEUTRALITY AND ANONYMITY

Introduction

In modern societies wide discretionary power and wide powers of delegated legislation are vested in administrators and it is held that the power thus conferred should only be used for the purposes for which they are conferred and for no other purposes.[160] It is expected from the civil servant to use the adjudicatory authority vested in them in free and fair manner without fear or favor. This discretionary power must be rationally used in impartial and neutral manner by giving due consideration to rules of laws. In practice however this does not happen neither the civil servant always remains neutral nor do the citizens in totality always desire them to be so.

The concept of anonymity by and large goes with concept of neutrality.

Concept of Neutrality

Max Weber- His contribution is outcome of his ideal bureaucracy. The bureaucracies have to

- Discharge impersonal officials obligation
- Be selected and promoted on merits.
- Act strictly according to rules and regulations.
- Such bureaucracies are politically neutral.

Fritz Morstein Marx

- Administrator does not have to indulge in ostrich like behaviors.

- Positively neutrality means working without reservation and with devotion for the success of or the political government.

- It is a two way phenomenon involving the political executives as well as the bureaucracy the political executive has to lay down the policy with the help of expertise of the bureaucracy, the bureaucracy on its part has to execute the policy without reservation even if its views have been considered and overruled.

British Concept of Neutrality

The political neutrality of the Civil Service is a fundamental feature of British democratic government and is essential for its efficient operation. There are two principles considered vital in this regard

i. In a democratic society it is desirable for all citizens to have a voice in the affairs of the State and for as many as possible to play an active part in public life. This is achieved by

   a. the free expression of a man's party-political views in private or through the ballot-box, this is a right universally exercised; and

   b. their expression in public for the purpose of propagating the ideas of a political party, in this case though it is also a right for the ordinary citizen but it is not a right which cannot justifiably be limited or withheld in certain circumstances by other considerations if these are sufficiently important to the public interest as a whole.

ii. The public interest demands the maintenance of political impartiality in the civil service and of confidence in that impartiality as an essential part of the structure of government.

The necessity of maintaining, without possibility of question, the public confidence in the political impartiality of the public service is axiomatic and cannot be disputed. The efficient and smooth working of democratic government depends very largely upon maintaining that confidence and on people believing that, notwithstanding political change, the civil service will give completely loyal service to the government of the day. The extension of the functions of the state has greatly increases the need for maintaining the impartiality of the service. Neutrality is based upon the assumption that this confidence must be maintained even at the cost of certain sacrifices. Entry into the civil service is a voluntary act and there can be no reasonable complaint if the conditions of service include some restrictions, as is the case in certain other professions and employments. The public interest demands, at least amongst those employees of the state who correspond with the common conception of the civil service, a manner of behaviour which is incompatible with the overt declaration of party political allegiance.[161]

American Concept of Neutrality

American conception of neutrality is reflected in 1955 Hoover commission's proposal to establish in the federal government a "senior civil service." These civil servants would be expected to exercise strict political neutrality; they would refrain from defending controversial policies before congress and from making other public statements which might taint them with partisanship and thus undermine their usefulness as civil servants.[162] The idea of neutrality in Hoover commission drew heavily on British conception.

Rationale

In Marxist conception, civil service is viewed as instrument of the ruling party. In the authoritarian single party rule, party itself is a personified state and civil service its stooge. This is not a universally accepted conception.

The basic assumptions behind the concept are-

- Product of merit system, secures apolitical public service hence is essential requirement for functioning of the multi party system.
- Advantages are permanence, continuity, reliability, and professionalism while disadvantages include conservatism,

devotion to routine and resistance to change. The advantages far weigh disadvantages.

- The alternative to neutral bureaucracy is spoils system.

Concept Challenged

- Neutrality was based on politics-administration dichotomy. In the modern times decision-making is no longer a prerogative of political executive. It has become a collective process involving political executives as well as professional civil service. The civil service being involved in complex and specialized policy making makes it politically susceptible.

- The civil service in developing countries is called upon to undertake the gigantic task of development administration that demands leadership, initiative, and engagement and also makes them involved in some sort of political process.

- The defining lines of policy formulation and policy implementation are always blurred.

- The political attachment to party may be abjured by neutrality but it cannot avoid professional and moral commitment to the development program.

- The political interference, discretionary powers, adjudicatory functions, role in policy, promotions, transfers and performance appraisal are issues that dabbles civil service into the area considered as politics. Further, the political angle gets reinforced by the self aggrandizing and complacent nature of civil servant.

- Neutrality if carried to extremes may lead to indifferent, unresponsive, rigid civil service.

Politicization of Bureaucracy

There are various studies that have analyzed the issue of the extent of politicization of civil services in various countries. In these studies they have made use of certain measures of neutrality, they are as follows

- The degree of influence in decision making
- The degree of segregating of the political executive from bureaucracy.
- The extent of political interference in the administrative work.
- The degree of its involvement in politics.
- The extent of confidence bureaucracy enjoys with the public.

Politicization of bureaucracy means the bureaucracy which is involved in or influences or influenced to any degree consciously or unconsciously by overt or by covert action is political it may because of its relation with political party in power or in opposition. These types of bureaucracies are classified according to the degree of politicization.

- Di-politicized bureaucracy: Political act of any nature and degree not allowed
- Semi -Politicized Bureaucracy: Allowed after retirement
- Committed bureaucracy- Policy of politic
- Fully politicized Bureaucracy – Follow the neutrality notion of political party

Politicization and Traditions of Administration- To maintain balance between the rights of civil servant as a citizen and need for impartiality in public work, politicization needs to be addressed, different countries have resolved this problem differently.

Anglo-American tradition of administration includes the countries having history of political neutrality, like UK, New Zealand, Canada, United States, etc. These countries are also affected by degree and variety of politicization. In Napoleonic tradition of administration countries traditionally have been more accepting of political influence over appointments to the public service than in the Anglo-American systems. It is possible because of strong legal norms of administrative impartiality. The countries include France, Spain, Greece, etc. In the Scandinavian countries like Denmark and Sweden there are indications that the positions are becoming more politicized. The Netherlands and Belgium represent the intersection of the German tradition and some exclusive features of the Napoleonic tradition. Belgium has had more of the French style of a political civil service. The Netherlands has had a less overtly political public service as in the two Anglo-Saxon countries, and that is also evident in the manner of politicization in the Netherlands. The top civil service in Germany has long offered opportunities to the 'political civil servant'- a senior official who is publicly associated with a political party but who will have worked up through the career system on a merit basis. Even though politicization is well established in the system, there has been some increase in the role of politics in appointments.[163]

Anonymity

The principles of 'Neutrality' and 'Anonymity' were evolved in British civil service during 1854 to 1916. It has been the hallmark of Whitehall model. Chadwick has said that, *neutrality would have been meaningless...anonymity impossible.* It flows directly from the doctrine of ministerial responsibility. Fits well with doctrine of Neutrality who is neutral have to act according to impersonal application of rules and regulations and hence has to act anonymously. Anonymity had been a cardinal principle of civil services and it has been enjoyed by them ever since. The advice imparted to minister is confidential. In the parliamentary democracy the convention of ministerial responsibility insulates civil servants from accountability. It is the minister who is responsible for all the actions to the legislature. The civil service traditionally has been protected also to enhance integrity and impartiality.

REFERENCES

1) **Herman Finer,** *The Theory and Practice of Modern Government,* Methuen and Co., 1932, P.723

2) **Ordway Tead and Henry C. Metcalf,** *Personnel Administration: Its Principles and Practice,* McGraw-Hill Book Company, New York, 1920, P.2

3) **Paul Van Riper,** *History of the United States Civil Service,* Harper Collins, New York, 1958, P.8

4) **Frederick Mosher,** *Democracy and the Public Service,* Oxford University Press, New York, 1982, P.86

5) National Academy of Public Administration, *The 21st Century Federal Manager: A Study of Changing Roles and Competencies,* Washington, D.C., 2002, P. 11

6) **R. Legge,** *HRM: Rhetoric, Reality and Hidden Agendas*, in J. Storey (ed.), *New Perspectives in Human Resources Management,* Routledge, London, 1992, P.57

7) **Michael Armstrong,** *A Handbook of Personnel Management Practice*, Kogan page, London, 1995

8) **O. Glenn Stahl,** *Public Personnel Administration,* Oxford and IBH Publishing, Calcutta, 1966, P.146

9) **Ismar Baruch,** *Position Classification in the Public Service: A report submitted to the civil service assembly by the committee on position-classification and pay-plans in the*

public service, Civil Service Assembly of the United States and Canada, Chicago, 1941.

10) **Leonard D. White,** *Introduction to the study of public administration,* Macmillan, New York, 1955, p.353

11) **O. Glenn Stahl,** *Public Personnel Administration,* Oxford and IBH Publishing, Calcutta, 1966, P.152-153

12) **O. Glenn Stahl,** *Public Personnel Administration,* Oxford and IBH Publishing, Calcutta, 1966, P.153-161

13) **Fred Telford,** *The Classification and Salary Standardization Movement in the Public Service,* The Annals of the American Academy of Political and Social Science, Vol. 113, May, 1924, PP. 206-215

14) **Marshall Edward Dimock, Gladys Gouverneur Ogden Dimock, Louis William Koenig,** *Public Administration,* Rinehart, USA, 1958, P.282

15) **J.D. Kingsley,** *Recruiting applicants for the public service,* a report submitted to the civil service assembly by the committee on recruiting applicants for the public service, Civil Service Assembly of the United States and Canada, Chicago, 1942, P.13

16) **William Doyle,** *Venality: The Sale of Offices in Eighteenth-Century France,* Clarendon Press Oxford, 1997

17) http://www.encyclopedia.com/topic/Patronage.aspx

18) **Dale S. Beach,** *Personnel: the management of people at work,* Macmillan, USA, 1980, P.358

19) **Edwin B. Flippo,** *Personnel Management,* McGraw- Hill, USA, 1980, P.181

20) **Ralph Assheton,** *Report of the committee on the training of civil servants,* H.M. Stationery office, London, 1944

21) **William G. Torpey,** *Public Personnel Management,* D Van Nostrand Company, USA, 1953, P.154

22)https://cosmolearning.org/documentaries/seduction-of-a-generation-sensitivity-training-as-brainwashing-1969/

23) http://www.imdb.com/title/tt1272785/

24) **O. Glenn Stahl,** *Public Personnel Administration,* Oxford and IBH Publishing, Calcutta, 1966, P.277

25)http://www.merriam-webster.com/dictionary/

26) American Heritage Dictionary of the English Language, Houghton Mifflin Harcourt Publishing Company, 2011

27) **O. Glenn Stahl,** *Public Personnel Administration,* Oxford and IBH Publishing, New Delhi, 1975, P.51

28) **Moorhead and Griffin,** *Organizational Behaviour: Managing People and Organizations,* Houghton Mifflin and Company, Canada, 1995

29) **E.H. Erikson,** *Childhood and Society,* Norton, New York, 1963

30) **D. T. Hall,** *Careers in Organizations,* Goodyear, California, 1976

31) **E. F. Huse and T.G. Cummings,** *Organization Development and Change,* West Publishing Company, New York, 1980

32) **G. W. Dalton, P.H. Thompson and R.L. Price,** *The Four Stages of Professional Career: A New Look at Performance by Professionals,* Organizational Dynamics, 1977, vol.6, PP. 19-42.

33) **Carl Heyel,** *The Encyclopedia of Management,* Reinhold Publishing Co., USA, 1982, P.835

34) **V.K. Rowland,** *Evaluating and Improving Managerial Performance,* McGraw-Hill, New York, 1970, P.210

35)http://www.businessdictionary.com/definition/performance-appraisal.html

36)http://www.etymonline.com/index.php?allowed_in_frame=0&search=promote

37) **L. D. White,** *Introduction to the Study of Public Administration,* Eurasia Publishing House, Delhi, 1968, P.400

38) **W. F. Willoughby,** *Principles of Public Administration,* Central Book Depot, Allahabad, 1953, P.274

39) Report of Committee on pay, etc., of State servants, H.M. Stationery off., London, 1923

40) Minutes of evidence taken before the royal commission on the civil service, 1929-31, H.M. Stationery off., London, PP.83-84

41) **Dr. L. D White,** *Introduction to the Study of Public Administration,* Macmillan, 1926, P.337 in A. R. Tyagi, *Public Administration- Principles and Practices*, Atma Ram and Sons, 1990, P.523

42)https://india.gov.in/spotlight/national-pension-system-retirement-plan-all

43) http://www.pensionersportal.gov.in/ClassOfPen.asp

44) http://www.pensionersportal.gov.in/retire-benefit.asp

45) http://pfrda.org.in/index.cshtml

46) http://pfrda.org.in/index1.cshtml?lsid=86

47) http://www.merriam-webster.com/dictionary/discipline

48)http://dictionary.cambridge.org/dictionary/english/discipline

49) **O. Glenn Stahl,** *Public Personnel Administration,* Oxford and IBH Publishing, New Delhi, 1975, P.110

50) **P.G. Aquinas,** *Human Resource Management-Principles and Practice,* Vikas Publishing House, New Delhi, 2009, P.219

51) **O. Glenn Stahl,** *Public Personnel Administration,* Oxford and IBH Publishing, New Delhi, 1975, P.315-316

52) **Paul John William Pigors, Charles Andrew Myers,** *Personnel Administration: A point of view and a method,* McGraw-Hill, 1973, P.325

53) **Paul John William Pigors, Charles Andrew Myers,** *Personnel Administration: A point of view and a method,* McGraw-Hill, 1973, P.161

54) Statistical Year Book, Ministry of Statistics and Programme Implementation, Government of India, http://mospi.nic.in/mospi_new/upload/statistical_year_book_20 11/SECTOR-6

55) National Study: India, International Labour Organization,http://www.ilo.org/wcmsp5/groups/public/---ed_dialogue/dialogue/documents/genericdocument/wcms_2053 65.pdf

56) Statistical Year Book, Ministry of Statistics and Programme Implementation, Government of India, http://mospi.nic.in/mospi_new/upload/statistical_year_book_20 11/SECTOR-6

57) **H.N. Mitra (Ed.),** The Indian Annual Register 1919-1947, Vol-I, 1920, Gyan Publishing House, New Delhi, P.231

58) Statistical Year Book, Ministry of Statistics and Programme Implementation, Government of India, http://mospi.nic.in/mospi_new/upload/statistical_year_book_20 11/SECTOR-6

59) http://www.itgoa.org/teamConstitution.php

60) http://auditflag.blogspot.in/

61) **W. Willard Wirtz,** *Public Employment and Public Policy,* in Stanley, Lieberman and Moskow (Ed.), Readings on Collective Negotiations in Public Education, Rand McNally, Chicago, 1967, P.5

62) **Gordon T. Nesvig,** *The New Dimensions of the Strike Question,* 28 Public Administration Review, 1967, P.26

63) **Marc J. Bloch,** *Public Employees' Right to Strike,* Cleveland State Law Review, CSU, USA, May 1969, P.396-397

64) **J. H. Macrae-Gibson,** The Whitley system in the civil service, The Fabian Society, London, 1922, PP.5,6,11,12

65) **J. H. Macrae-Gibson,** The Whitley system in the civil service, The Fabian Society, London, 1922, PP.40,41

66) Alternate dispute resolution handbook, Office of Personnel Management, United States, www.opm.gov/policy-data-oversight/employee-reltions/Employeerightsappeals/alternative disputeresolution/handbook.pdf

67)http://persmin.gov.in/DOPT/RTICorner/ProactiveDisclosure/FAQ_JCA.pdf

68)http://www.etymonline.com/index.php?term=bureau

69) **Fred Riggs,** *Introduction: Shifting meanings of term 'bureaucracy',* In search of rational organization, International Social Science Journal, UNESCO, Vol. XXXI, No. 4, 1979, P. 563

70) **J. S. Mill,** *Considerations on Representative Government,* Parker, Son, & Bourn, London, 1861, P. 113

71) **Harold Laski,** *Bureaucracy,* Encyclopaedia of the Social Sciences, Vol. 3. New York, Macmillan. 1930, P.70

72) **Martin Albrow,** *Bureaucracy,* Praeger, New York, 1970, P.92

73) **Lasswell and Kaplan,** *Power and Society: A Framework for Political Enquiry,* Yale University Press, New Haven, 1950, P.209

74) **J. S. Mill,** *On Liberty,* Longmans Green, London, 1892, P. 66

75) **Gaetano Mosca,** *The Ruling Class,* McGraw-Hill, New York, 1939, P. 80-87

76) **Robert Michels,** *Political Parties,* Dover Publications, New York, 1962, P. 186

77) **Ramsay Muir,** *Peers and Bureaucrats,* Constable and Company, London, 1910, P. 8, 14

78) **Walter R. Sharp,** *Le Développement de la Bureaucratie aux États-Unis,* Revue des Sciences Politiques,\o\. 50, 1927, P. 394 in **Fred Riggs,** *Introduction: Shifting meanings of term 'bureaucracy',* In search of rational organization, International Social Science Journal, UNESCO, Vol. XXXI, No. 4, 1979, P. 566

79) **Arnold Brecht,** *How Bureaucracies Develop and Function,* Annals of the American Academy of Political and Social Science, Vol. 292, 1954, P.1

80) **J. S. Mill,** *Principles of Political Economy, Parker,* London, 1848, P.528

81) **Eduard Fischel,** *Die Verfassung Englands* Schneider, Berlin, 1862, P.132-136 from Martin Albrow, *Bureaucracy,* Praeger, New York, 1970, P.24

82) **Robert Michels,** *Political Parties,* Dover Publications, New York, 1962, P.186

83) **F. von. Schulte,** *Bureaucracy and its Operation in Germany and Austria-Hungary,* Contemporary Review, Vol. 37, 1880, P. 458.

84) **Walter Bagehot,** *The English Constitution,* Fontana, London, 1963, P.197

85) **Max Weber,** *The Theory of Social and Economic Organization,* The Free Press, Glencoe, 111, Canada, 1947, P.552, translated by A.M. Henderson and Talcott Parsons

86) **Taylor Cole,** *The Canadian Bureaucracy,* Duke University Press, Durham, N.C., 1949, P.3

87) **Joseph LaPalombara (ed.),** *Bureaucracy and Political Development,* Princeton University Press, N.J., 1963, P.6-7

88) **Martin Albrow,** *Bureaucracy,* Praeger, New York, 1970, P.20

89) **Fritz Morstein Marx,** *The Administrative State,* University of Chicago Press, Chicago, 1957, P.20

90) **Reinhard Bendix**, *Bureaucracy,* International Encyclopaedia of the Social Sciences, Vol. II., Macmillan, New York, 1968, P.206

91) **Talcott Parsons,** *Structure and Process in Modern Societies,* The Free Press, Glencoe, 111, Canada, 1960, P.2

92) **Charles S. Hyneman,** *Bureaucracy in a Democracy,* Harper and Brothers, New York, 1950, P.3

93) **Karl A. Wittfogel,** *Oriental Despotism,* Yale University Press, New Haven, USA, 1957

94) **James Burnham,** *The Managerial Revolution,* Indiana University Press, Bloomington, USA, 1941

95) **Robert V. Presthus,** *The Organizational Society,* Knopf, New York, 1962, P.84

96) **Martin Albrow,** *Bureaucracy,* Praeger, New York, 1970, P.104

97) **Bruno Rizzi,** *La Bureaucratisation du Monde,* Paris, 1939

98) **Max Schachtman**, *The bureaucratic revolution: the rise of the Stalinist state,* Donald Press, New York, USA, 1962

99) **Milovan Djilas,** *The New Class,* Praeger, New York, 1957

100) **Karl Mannheim,** *Freedom, Power and Democratic Planning,* Routledge & Kegan Paul, London, 1951

101) **Honoré de Balzac,** *Les Employés,* 1836, P. 84

102) **Martin Albrow,** *Bureaucracy,* Praeger, New York, 1970, P.29

103) **Martin Albrow,** *Bureaucracy,* Praeger, New York, 1970, P.30

104) **Martin Albrow,** *Bureaucracy,* Praeger, New York, 1970, P.30, From F. LePlay, *La Réforme Sociale en France,* Pion, Paris, 1864, P.236

105) **Marshall E Dimock,** *Bureaucracy Examined,* Public Administration Review, Vol. 4, 1944, P. 198

106) **E. Strauss,** *The Ruling Servants,* Allen and Unwin, London, 1961, P.41

107) **Michel Crozier,** *The Bureaucratic Phenomenon,* University of Chicago Press, Chicago, 1964, P.3

108) **Fred Riggs,** *Introduction: Shifting meanings of term 'bureaucracy',* In search of rational organization, International Social Science Journal, UNESCO, Vol. XXXI, No. 4, 1979, P. 576

109) **Peter M. Blau,** *Bureaucracy in Modem Society,* Random House, New York, 1956, P.60

110) **G.R. Francis, R.C. Stone,** *Service and Procedure in Bureaucracy,* University of Minnesota Press, Minneapolis, 1956, P.3

111) **Peter Leonard,** *Sociology in Social Work,* Routledge and Kegan Paul, London, 1966, P.81

112) **Vikram Singh,** *Public Administration Dictionary,* Tata McGraw-Hill, India P.133

113) Collins English Dictionary- Complete and Unabridged, William Collins Sons and Co., 2012

114) Random House Dictionary, 2016

115) **Herman Finer,** *The Theory and Practice of Modern Government,* Methuen and Co., 1932

116) **Hans Rosenberg,** *Bureaucracy, Aristocracy, and Autocracy: The Prussian Experience 1660-1815,* Harvard University Press, 1958

117) **John R. Gillis,** *The Prussian Bureaucracy in Crisis, 1840-1860,* Stanford University Press, 1971

118) **Mark D. Bradbury, and J. Edward Kellough,** *Representative Bureaucracy: Exploring the Potential for Active Representation in Local Government,* Journal of Public Administration Research and Theory, Oxford University Press, 2007, 18, P. 697–714.

119) **Lindsey L. Evans,** *Enhancing Representation: Hispanic Minorities in 21st Century Public Service Delivery,* ASPA, 2014

120) **John J. Hindera,** *Representative Bureaucracy: Further Evidence of Active Representation in the EEOC District Offices,* Journal of Public Administration Research and Theory, Oxford University Press,1993, 3(4): P.417

121) **David Nachmias, David Rosenbloom**, *Bureaucratic Culture: Citizens and Administrators in Israel,* Croom Helm and St. Martin's Press, London and New York, 1978, PP.39,40,171

122) **Susan L. Moffitt,** *Making Policy Public- Participatory Bureaucracy in American Democracy,* Cambridge University Press, 2014, PP.28-54

123) **David Nachmias, David Rosenbloom**, *Bureaucratic Culture: Citizens and Administrators in Israel,* Croom Helm and St. Martin's Press, London and New York, 1978, PP.183-196

124) **Keith Taylor (ed, tr.),** *Henri de Saint Simon, 1760-1825: Selected writings on science, industry and social organization,* Holmes and Meier Publishers, New York, USA, 1975, PP. 158–161.

125) **Alan Ryan,** *On Politics: A History of Political Thought: From Herodotus to the Present* (II), Liveright, 2012. pp. 647–651

126)https://www.marxists.org/archive/marx/works/1843/critique-hpr/ch03.htm

127) **Martin Albrow,** *Bureaucracy,* Praeger, New York, 1970

128) **Martin Krygier,** *State and Bureaucracy in Europe: The growth of a concept,* in Eugene Kamenka and Martin Krygier,

Bureaucracy- The career of a concept, Arnold Heinemann Publishers, New Delhi, PP.3-10

129) **Eva Etzioni-Halevy,** *Bureaucracy and Democracy,* Routledge and Kegan Paul, London, 1983, PP.30-31

130) **Edgar Norman Gladden,** *Civil Service or Bureaucracy,* Staples Press, London, 1956, P.17

131) **Herman Finer,** *Theory and Practice of Modern Government,* Henry Holt and Co, New York, 1949, P.709

132) **Edward Bridges,** Encyclopaedia Britannica, http://www.britannica.com/topic/civil-service

133) Collins English Dictionary – Complete and Unabridged, Harper Collins Publishers, 12th Edition, 2014

134) Professor Peter Hennessy, Founder's Day address, Hawarden Castle, 8 July 1999, cited in *Whither the Civil Service,* Research Paper 03/49, House of Commons Library, May 2003

135) Part II, Clause 4, GOI orders/decisions, (4) classification of posts, Central Civil Services (Classification, Control and Appeal) Rules, 1965

-- *Cadre Review of Group 'A' Central Services- A Monograph,* Cadre Review Division, Department of Personnel and Training, Ministry of Personnel, Public Grievances and Pensions, Government of India, PP.4-6.

136) *Cadre Review of Group 'A' Central Services- A Monograph,* Cadre Review Division, Department of Personnel and Training, Ministry of Personnel, Public Grievances and Pensions, Government of India, PP.5-6.

137) *Cadre Review of Group 'A' Central Services- A Monograph,* Cadre Review Division, Department of Personnel and Training, Ministry of Personnel, Public Grievances and Pensions, Government of India, P.6.

138) www.haileybury.com

139) **Anthony Kirk- Greene,** *The Colonial Service Training Courses- Professionalizing the colonial service,* http://www.britishempire.co.uk/

140) http://www.lbsnaa.gov.in/

141) http://www.svpnpa.gov.in/

142) http://www.asci.org.in/

143) http://www.nird.org.in/

144) http://meafsi.gov.in/

145) http://www.ignfa.gov.in/

146) http://nacen.gov.in/

147) http://www.nadt.gov.in/

148) http://naaa.gov.in/

149) http://www.ies.gov.in/

150) http://www.iipa.org.in/

151)http://www.persmin.nic.in/DOPT/Publication/HandbookO nPersonnelOfficers/ch-18.pdf

152) Ministry of Home Affairs Office Memorandum No. 1/5/58-RPS dated 26-2-58.

153) Ministry of Home Affairs Office Memorandum No. 9/21158-RPS dated 10-6-59 read with Ministry of Home Affairs Office Memorandum No. 1/9 /66-Estt (D) dated 22-7-66.

154) Ministry of Home Affairs Office Memorandum No. 115/64-Estt(D) dated 14-4-64 read with Ministry of Home Affairs Office Memorandum No. 1/9/66-Estt(D) dated 22-7-66. 248 249

155) Ministry of Home Affairs Office Memorandum No. 1/13/58-RPS dated 28-10-58

156) Ministry of Home Affairs Office Memorandum No. 1/1/55-RPS dated 17-2-55 sub-para 1(ii)

157)http://performance.gov.in/sites/default/files/document/PA R/Review

158) **Robert Presthus,** *Decline of the Generalist Myth,* Public Administration Review, Vol. 24, Nov- Dec, 1964

159) **Yehezkel Dror,** *'Specialists vs. Generalists'- A Miss-Question,* RAND Corporation, Doc.No: P-3997, USA, 1968

160) State of Bombay v. K.P. Krishnan, AIR 1960 SC1223

161) **Mr. J. C. Masterman (Chairman),** *Report of the Committee on the Political Activities of Civil Servants,* His Majesty's Stationery Office, London, June,1949

162) **Herbert J. Storing, Joseph M. Bessette,** *Toward a More Perfect Union: Writings of Herbert J. Storing,* American Enterprise Institute, Washington D.C., USA, 1995, P.317

163) **B. Guy Peters and Jon Pierre (Ed.),** *Politicization of the Civil Service in Comparative Perspective: The quest for Control,* Routledge, London, 2004, P.9-11